SEMIOTEXT(E) INTERVENTION SERIES

© 2010 by Tiqqun. Originally published by Éditions La
Fabrique in 2009.
This translation © 2010 by Semiotext(e)

Published by Semiotext(e)
2007 Wilshire Blvd., Suite 427, Los Angeles, CA 90057
www.semiotexte.com

Thanks to John Ebert.

Design: Hedi El Kholti

ISBN: 978-1-58435-086-6
Distributed by The MIT Press, Cambridge, Mass.
and London, England
Printed in the United States of America

Tiqqun

Introduction to Civil War

Translated by Alexander R. Galloway & Jason E. Smith

semiotext(e)
intervention
series □ 4

Contents

A Note on the Translation

Introduction à la guerre civile (*Introduction to Civil War*) and *Comment faire?* (*How Is It to Be Done?*) first appeared in issue number two of the journal *Tiqqun* published in France in September, 2001. *Introduction à la guerre civile* was reprinted as a book by VLCP in 2006. In 2009 La Fabrique reprinted both texts as part of the volume *Contributions à la guerre en cours*.

The works do not bear a normal author attribution. Articles published in *Tiqqun* 2 are anonymous, and the issue itself does not contain a listing of its editorial committee. "Tiqqun" can here refer to an anonymous collective, the journal in which these texts appeared, a subjective process, or to the historical process to which these same texts bear witness.

All notes are ours. We have tried to use them sparingly so as not to distract from the text.

We wish to thank Joshua Jordan and Youna Kwak for their invaluable contributions to the translation.

— Alexander R. Galloway and Jason E. Smith

Introduction to Civil War

We decadents have frayed nerves. Everything, or almost everything, wounds us, and what doesn't will likely be irritating. That's why we make sure no one ever touches us. We can only stand smaller and smaller—these days, nanometric—doses of truth, and much prefer long gulps of its antidote instead. Images of happiness, tried and true sensations, kind words, smooth surfaces, familiar feelings and the innermost intimacy, in short, narcosis by the pound and above all: no war, above all, no war. The best way to put it is that this whole preemptive, amniotic environment boils down to a desire for a *positive anthropology*. We need THEM to tell us what "man" is, what "we" are, what we are allowed to want and to be. Ultimately, our age is fanatical about a lot of things, and especially about the question of MAN, through which ONE[1] sublimates away the undeniable fact of Bloom.[2] This anthropology, insofar as it is dominant, is not only positive by virtue of an irenic, slightly vacuous and gently pious conception of human nature. It is positive first and foremost because it assigns "Man" qualities, determined attributes and substantial predicates. This is why even the pessimist anthropology of the Anglo-Saxons, with its hypostasis of interests, needs and the *struggle for life* plays a reassuring role, for it still offers some practicable convictions concerning the essence of man.

But we—those of us who refuse to settle for any sort of comfort, we who admittedly have frayed nerves but also intend to make them still more resistant, still more unyielding—we need something else entirely. We need a *radically negative* anthropology, we need a few abstractions that are just empty enough, just transparent enough to prevent our usual prejudices, a *physics* that holds in store, for each being, its disposition toward the miraculous. Some concepts that crack the ice in order to attain, or *give rise to*, experience. To make ourselves handle it.

There is nothing we can say about men, that is, about their coexistence, that would not immediately act as a tranquillizer. The impossibility of predicting anything about this relentless freedom forces us to designate it with an undefined term, a blind word, that ONE has the habit of using to name whatever ONE knows nothing about, because ONE does not *want* to understand it, or understand *that the world cannot do without us*. The term is *civil war*. This move is tactical; we want to reappropriate, in advance, the term by which our operations will be *necessarily covered*.

**Civil War,
Forms-of-life**

Whoever does not take sides in a civil war is struck with infamy, and loses all right to politics.

— Solon, *The Constitution of Athens*

1 The elementary human unity is not the *body*—the individual—but the form-of-life.

2 The form-of-life is not *beyond* bare life, it is its intimate polarization.[3]

3 Each body is affected by its form-of-life as if by a clinamen, a leaning, an attraction, a *taste*. A body leans toward whatever leans its way. This goes for each and every situation. Inclinations go both ways.

GLOSS: To the inattentive observer, it may seem that Bloom offers a counterexample: a body deprived of every penchant and inclination, and immune to all attractions. But on closer inspection, it is clear that Bloom refers less to an absence of taste than to a special *taste for absence*. Only this penchant can account for all the efforts Bloom makes to *persevere* in Bloom, to keep what leans his way at a distance, in order to *decline* all experience. Like the religious, who, unable to oppose *another worldliness* to "this world," must convert their absence within the world into a critique of worldliness *in general*, Bloom tries to flee from a world that has no outside. In every situation he responds with the same disengagement, each time slipping away from the situation. Bloom is therefore a body distinctively affected by a *proclivity toward nothingness*.

4 This taste, this clinamen, can either be warded off or embraced. To take on a form-of-life is not simply to know a penchant: it means to *think* it. I call *thought* that which converts a form-of-life into a *force*, into a sensible effectivity.

In every situation there is one line that stands out among all the others, the line along which *power grows*. Thought is the capacity for singling out and following this line. A form-of-life can be embraced only by following this line, meaning that: *all thought is strategic.*

GLOSS: To latecomer's eyes like ours, the conjuring away of every form-of-life seems to be the West's peculiar destiny. Paradoxically, in this civilization that we can no longer claim as our own without consenting to self-liquidation, conjuring away forms-of-life most often appears as a *desire for form*: the search for an archetypal resemblance, an Idea of self placed before or in front of oneself. Admittedly, this *will to identity*, wherever it has been fully expressed, has had the hardest time masking the icy nihilism and the aspiration to nothingness that forms its spine.

But the conjuring away of forms-of-life also has a minor, more cunning form called *consciousness* and, at its highest point, *lucidity*—two "virtues" THEY prize all the more because these virtues render bodies increasingly powerless. At that point, ONE starts to call "lucidity" the knowledge of this weakness that offers no way out.

Taking on a form-of-life is completely different from the striving of the consciousness or the will, or from the effects of either.

Actually, to assume a form-of-life is a letting-go, an abandonment. It is at once fall and elevation, a movement and a staying-within-oneself.

5 "My" form-of-life relates not to *what* I am, but to *how* I am what I am.

GLOSS: This statement performs a slight shift. A slight shift in the direction of a taking leave of metaphysics. Leaving metaphysics is not a philosophical imperative, but a physiological necessity. Having now reached the endpoint of its deployment, metaphysics gathers itself into a planetary injunction to absence. What Empire demands is not that each conforms to a common law, but that each conforms to its own particular identity. Imperial power depends on the adherence of bodies to their supposed qualities or predicates in order to leverage control over them.

"My" form-of-life does not relate to *what* I am, but to *how*, to the specific *way*, I am what I am. In other words, between a being and its qualities, there is the abyss of its own presence and the singular experience *I* have of it, at a certain place and time. Unfortunately for Empire, the form-of-life animating a body is not to be found in any of its predicates—big, white, crazy, rich, poor, carpenter, arrogant, woman, or French—but in the singular *way* of its presence, in the irreducible event of its being-in-situation. And it is precisely where predication is most violently applied—in the rank domain of morality—that its failure fills us with joy: when, for example, we come across a completely abject being whose *way* of being abject nevertheless touches us in such a way that any repulsion within us is snuffed out, and in this way proves to us that *abjection itself is a quality*.

To embrace a form-of-life means being more faithful to our penchants than to our predicates.

6 Asking why this body is affected by this form-of-life rather than another is as meaningless as asking why there is something rather than nothing. Such a question betrays only a rejection, and sometimes a fear, of undergoing contingency. And, *a fortiori*, a refusal even to acknowlege it.

GLOSS α: A better question would be to ask *how* a body takes on substance, how a body becomes *thick*, how it *incorporates* experience. Why do we sometimes undergo heavy polarizations with far-reaching effects, and at other times weak, superficial ones? How can we extract ourselves from this dispersive mass of Bloomesque bodies, from this global Brownian motion where the most vital bodies proceed from one petty abandonment to the next, from one attenuated form-of-life to another, consistently following a principle of prudence—never get carried away, beyond a certain level of intensity? In other words, how could these bodies have become so *transparent*?

GLOSS β: The most Bloomesque notion of freedom is the freedom of *choice*, understood as a methodical abstraction from every situation. This concept of freedom forms the most effective antidote against every real freedom. The only substantial freedom is to follow right to the end, to the point where it vanishes, the line along which power grows for a certain form-of-life. This raises our capacity to then be affected by other forms-of-life.

7 A body's persistence in letting a *single* form-of-life affect it, despite the diversity of situations it passes through, depends on its crack. The more a body cracks up—that is, the wider and deeper its crack becomes—the fewer the polarizations compatible with its survival there are, and the more it will tend to recreate situations in which it finds itself involved in its familiar polarizations. The bigger a body's crack grows, the more its absence to the world increases and its penchants dwindle.

GLOSS: Form-of-life means therefore that my relation to myself is only one *part* of my relation to the world.

8 The experience one form-of-life has of another is not communicable to the latter, even if it can be translated; and we all know what happens with translations. Only facts can be made clear: behaviors, attitudes, assertions—*gossip*. Forms-of-life do not allow for neutral positions, they offer no safe haven for a universal observer.

GLOSS: To be sure, there is no lack of candidates vying to reduce all forms-of-life to the Esperanto of objectified "cultures," "styles," "ways of life" and other relativist mysteries. What these wretches are up to is, however, no mystery: they want to make us play the grand, one-dimensional game of identities and differences. This is the expression that the most rabid hostility toward forms-of-life takes.

9 In and of themselves, forms-of-life can be neither said nor described. They can only be shown—each time, in an always singular context. On the other hand, considered locally, the play between them obeys rigorous signifying mechanisms. If they are thought, these determinisms are transformed into *rules* which can then be amended. Each sequence of play is bordered, on either edge, by an *event*. The event disorders the play between forms-of-life, introduces a fold within it, suspends past determinisms and inaugurates new ones through which it must be reinterpreted. In all things, we start with and from the middle.

GLOSS α: The distance required for the description *as such* of a form-of-life is, precisely, the distance of enmity.

GLOSS β: Every attempt to grasp a "people" as a form-of-life—as race, class, ethnicity, or nation—has been undermined by the fact that the ethical differences *within* each "people" have always been greater than the ethical differences between "peoples" themselves.

10 Civil war is the free play of forms-of-life; it is the principle of their coexistence.

11 War, because in each singular play between forms-of-life, the possibility of a fierce confrontation—the possibility of violence—can *never* be discounted.

Civil, because the confrontation between forms-of-life is not like that between States—a coincidence between a population and a territory—but like the confrontation between *parties*, in the sense this word had before the advent of the modern State. And because we must be precise from now on, we should say that forms-of-life confront one another as *partisan war machines.*

Civil war, then, because forms-of-life know no separation between men and women, political existence and bare life, civilians and military;

because whoever is neutral *is still a party* to the free play of forms-of-life;

because this play between forms-of-life has no beginning or end that can be *declared*, its only possible end being a physical end of the world that precisely no one would be able to declare;

and above all because I know of no body that does not get hopelessly carried away in the excessive, and perilous, course of the world.

GLOSS α: "Violence" is something new in history. We decadents are the first to know this curious thing: *violence*. Traditional societies knew of theft, blasphemy, parricide, abduction, sacrifice, insults and revenge. Modern States, beyond the dilemma of adjudicating facts, recognized only infractions of the Law and the penalties administered to rectify them. But they certainly knew plenty about foreign wars and, within their borders, the authoritarian disciplining of bodies. In fact, only the timid atom of imperial society— Bloom—thinks of "violence" as a radical and unique evil lurking behind countless masks, an evil which it is so vitally important to identify, in order to eradicate it all the more thoroughly. For us, ultimately, violence is *what has been taken from us*, and today we need to take it back.

When Biopower starts speaking about traffic accidents as "violence on the highways," we begin to realize that for imperial society the term violence only refers to its own vocation for death. This society has forged this negative concept of violence in order to reject anything within it that might still carry a certain intensity or charge. In an increasingly explicit way, imperial society, in all its details, experiences itself *as violence*. When this society hunts down violence everywhere, it does nothing other than express its own desire to *pass away*.

GLOSS β: ONE finds speaking of civil war repugnant. But when ONE does it anyway, they assign it a circumscribed place and time. Hence you have the "civil war in France" (1871), in Spain (1936–39), the civil war in Algeria and maybe soon in Europe. At this point one should mention that the French, exhibiting the emasculation that comes so naturally to them, translate the American "Civil War" as "The War of Secession." They do so to demonstrate their determination to side unconditionally with the victor whenever the victor is also the State. The only way to lose this habit of giving civil war a beginning, end and territorial limit—this habit of making it an exception to the normal order of things rather than considering its infinite metamorphoses in time and space—is to shine a light on the sleight of hand it covers up.

Remember how those who wanted to suppress the guerilla war in Columbia in the early '60s preemptively gave the name "la Violencia" (the Violence) to the historical period they wanted to close out?

12 The point of view of civil war is the point of view of the political.

13 When, at a certain time and place, two bodies affected by the same form-of-life meet, they experience an objective pact, which precedes any decision. They experience *community*.

GLOSS: The deprivation of such an experience in the West has caused it to be haunted by the old metaphysical phantasm of the "human community"—also known under the name *Gemeinwesen* by currents working in the wake of Amadeo Bordiga. The Western intellectual is so far removed from any access to a real community that he has to confect this amusing little fetish: the human community. Whether he wears the Nazi-humanist uniform of "human nature" or the hippy rags of anthropology, whether he withdraws into a community whose power has been carefully disembodied, a purely potential community, or dives head-first into the less subtle concept of "total" man—through which all human predicates would be totalized—it is always the same terror that is expressed: the terror of having to think one's singular, determined, *finite* situation; this terror seeks refuge in the reassuring fantasy of totality or earthly unity. The resulting abstraction might be called the multitude, global civil society or the human species. What's important is not the name, but the operation performed. All the recent inanities about THE cyber-communist community or THE cyber-total man would not have gotten off the ground without a certain strategic opportunity that opened up at the very moment a worldwide movement was forming to refute it. Let's remember that sociology was born at the very moment the most irreconcilable conflict ever witnessed—the class struggle—emerged at the heart of the social, and this discipline was born in the very country where the struggle was most violent, in France in the second half of the nineteenth century. It was born as a response to this struggle.

Today, when "society" is nothing more than a hypothesis, and hardly the most plausible one at that, any claim to defend this society against the supposed fascism lurking in every form of community is nothing more than a rhetorical exercise steeped in bad faith. Who, after all, still speaks of "society" other than the citizens of Empire, who have come or rather *huddled* together against the self-evidence of Empire's final implosion, against the ontological obviousness of civil war?

14 There is no community except in singular relations. *The* community doesn't exist. There is only community, community that circulates.

GLOSS α: Community never refers to a collection of bodies conceived independently of their world. It refers to the nature of the relations between these bodies and between these bodies and their world. The moment community tries to incarnate itself in an isolatable subject, in a distinct, separate reality, the moment it tries to materialize the separation between what is inside it and what is outside, it confronts its own impossibility. This point of impossibility is communion. In communion, the complete self-presence of the community coincides with the dissipation of all community within singular relations, and therefore coincides with its tangible absence.

GLOSS β: All bodies are in movement. Even when it is immobile, a body still comes into presence, puts into play the world it bears, and follows its fate. Certain bodies *go together*. They tend toward one another, lean on one another: there is community among them. Others flee one another, don't go together, and clash. Within the community of each form-of-life there are also communities of things and gestures, communities of habits and affects, a community of thoughts. It goes without saying that bodies deprived of community also have no *taste*: they do not see that certain things go together, while others do not.

15 There can be no community *of those who are there.*

GLOSS: Every community is both *an actuality and a potentiality*. When it claims to be completely realized, as in Total Mobilization, or remain pure potentiality, as in the heavenly solitude of Bloom—*there is no* community.

16 When I encounter a body affected by the same form-of-life as I am, this is community, and it puts me in *contact* with my own power.

17 *Sense* is the element of the Common, that is, every event, as an irruption of sense, institutes a common.

The body that says "I," in truth says "we."

A gesture or statement endowed with sense carves a *determined* community out of a mass of bodies, a community that must itself be taken on in order to take on this gesture or statement.

18 When two bodies animated by forms-of-life that are absolutely foreign to one another meet at a certain moment and in a certain place, they experience *hostility*. This type of encounter gives rise to no relation; on the contrary, it bears witness to the original absence of relation.

The hostis can be identified and its situation can be known, but it *itself* cannot be known for what it is, that is, *in its singularity*. Hostility is therefore the impossibility for bodies that don't go together to know one another as singular.

Whenever a thing is known in its singularity, it takes leave of the sphere of hostility and thereby becomes a friend—or an enemy.

19 For me, the hostis is a nothing that demands to be annihilated, either through a cessation of hostility, or by ceasing to exist altogether.

20 A hostis can be annihilated, but the sphere of hostility itself cannot be reduced to nothing. The imperial humanist who flatters himself by declaring "nothing human is foreign to me" only reminds us how far he had to go to become so foreign *to himself.*

21 Hostility is practiced in many ways, by different methods and with varied results. The commodity or contractual relation, slander, rape, insult, and pure and simple destruction all take their places side-by-side as practices of *reduction*: even THEY understand this. Other forms of hostility take more perverse and less obvious paths. Consider potlatch, praise, politeness, prudence or even hospitality. These are all what ONE rarely recognizes as so many practices of *abasement*, as indeed they are.

GLOSS: In his *Le vocabulaire des institutions indo-européennes*, Benveniste was incapable of explaining why the Latin word *hostis* could simultaneously signify "foreigner," "enemy," "host," "guest," and "he who has the same rights as the Roman people," or even, "he who is bound to me through potlatch," i.e. the *forced* reciprocity of the gift.[4] It is nevertheless clear that whether it be the sphere of law, the laws of hospitality, flattening someone beneath a pile of gifts or an armed offensive, there are many ways to *erase* the hostis, of making sure he does not become a singularity for me. That is how I keep the hostis foreign. It is our weakness that keeps us from admitting this. The third article of Kant's *Towards Perpetual Peace*, which proposes the conditions for a final dissolution of particular communities and their subsequent formal reintegration into a Universal State, is nevertheless unequivocal in insisting that "Cosmopolitan right shall be limited to conditions of universal *hospitality*."[5] And just recently, didn't Sebastian Roché, that unacknowledged creator of the idea of "incivility" and French fanatic of zero tolerance, that hero of the impossible Republic, didn't he give his most recent (March 2000) book the utopian title *The Society of Hospitality*?[6] Does Sebastian Roché read Kant, Hobbes and the pages of *France-Soir*, or does he simply read the mind of the French Interior Minister?

22 Anything we usually blanket with the name "indifference" does not exist. If I do not know a form-of-life and if it is therefore nothing to me, then I am *not even indifferent* to it. If I do know it and it exists for me *as if* it did not exist, it is in this case quite simply and clearly *hostile* for me.

23 Hostility distances me from my own power.

24 Between the extremes of community and hostility lies the sphere of friendship and enmity. Friendship and enmity are ethico-political concepts. That they both give rise to an intense circulation of affects only demonstrates that affective realities are works of art, that the play between forms-of-life can be *elaborated*.

GLOSS α: In the stockpile of instruments deployed by the West against all forms of community, one in particular has occupied, since around the twelfth century, a privileged and yet unsuspected place. I am speaking of the concept of *love*. We should acknowledge that the false alternative it has managed to impose on everything— "do you love me, or not?"—has been incredibly effective in masking, repressing, and crushing the whole gamut of highly differentiated affects and all the crisply defined degrees of intensity that can arise when bodies come into contact. In this set of false alternatives, love has functioned as a way to reduce the extreme possibility of an elaborate working out of the play among forms-of-life. Undoubtedly, the ethical poverty of the present, which amounts to a kind of permanent coercion into coupledom, is due largely to this concept of love.

GLOSS β: To give proof, it would be enough to recall how, through the entire process of "civilization," the criminalization of all sorts of passions accompanied the sanctification of love as the one true passion, as the passion par excellence.

GLOSS γ: All this of course goes only for the notion of love, not for all those things it has given rise to, despite itself. I am speaking not only of certain momentous perversions, but also of that little projectile "I love you," which is *always* an event.

25 I am bound to the friend by some experience of election, understanding or *decision* that implies that the growth of his power entails the growth of my own. Symmetrically, I am bound to the enemy by election, only this time a disagreement that, in order for my power to grow, implies that I confront him, that I undermine his forces.

GLOSS: This was the brilliant reply of Hannah Arendt to a Zionist who, after the publication of *Eichmann in Jerusalem* and during the subsequent scandal, reproached her for not loving the people of Israel: "I don't love peoples. I only love my friends."

26 What is at stake in confronting the enemy is never its existence, only its power, its potentiality.

Not only can an annihilated enemy no longer recognize its own defeat, it always ends up coming back to *haunt* us, first as a ghost and later as *hostis*.

27 All differences among forms-of-life are *ethical* differences. These differences authorize play, in *all* its forms. These kinds of play are not political in themselves, but become political at a certain level of intensity, that is, when they have been *elaborated to a certain degree*.

GLOSS: We reproach this world not for going to war too ferociously, nor for trying to prevent it by all means; we only reproach it for reducing war *to its most empty and worthless forms*.

28 I am not going to demonstrate the permanence of civil war with a starry-eyed celebration of the most beautiful episodes of social war, or by cataloguing all those moments when class antagonism achieved its finest expressions. I am not going to talk about the English, Russian or French revolutions, the Makhnovshchina, the Paris Commune, Gracchus Babeuf, May '68 or even the Spanish Civil War. Historians will be grateful: their livelihoods aren't threatened. My method is more twisted. I will show *how* civil war continues even when it is said to be absent or provisionally brought under control. My task will be to display the means used by the relentless process of depoliticization that begins in the Middle Ages and continues up to today, just when, as we all know, "everything is political" (Marx). In other words, the whole will not be grasped by connecting the dots between historical summits, but by following a low-level, unbroken, existential sequence.

GLOSS: If the end of the Middle Ages is sealed by the splitting of the ethical element into two autonomous spheres, morality and politics, the end of "Modern Times" is marked by the reunification of these two abstract domains—*as separate*. This reunification gave us our new tyrant: THE SOCIAL.

29 *Naming* can take two mutually hostile forms. One wards something off, the other embraces it. Empire speaks of "civil wars" just as the Modern State did, but it does so in order to better control the masses of those who will give anything to avert civil war. I myself speak of "civil war," and even refer to it as a foundational fact. But I speak of civil war in order to embrace it and *to raise it to its highest forms*. In other words: according to my taste.

30 I call "communism" the real movement that elaborates, everywhere and at every moment, civil war.

31 At the outset, my own objective will not be obvious. For those familiar with it, it will be felt everywhere, and it will be completely absent for those who don't know a thing about it. Anyway, programs are only good for putting off what they claim to promote. Kant's criterion for a maxim's morality was that its public formulation not prevent its realization. My own moral ambitions will therefore not exceed the following formulation: *spread a certain ethic of civil war, a certain art of distances.*

The Modern State,
The Economic Subject

The history of state formation in Europe
is a history of the neutralization of
differences—denominational, social,
and otherwise—within the state.

— Carl Schmitt, "Neutralität und
Neutralisierungen"

32 The modern State is not defined as a set of institutions whose different arrangements would provide a stimulating pluralism. The modern State, insofar as it still exists, defines itself *ethically* as the theater of operations for a twofold fiction: the fiction that when it comes to forms-of-life both neutrality and centrality can exist.

GLOSS: We can recognize the fragile formations of power by their relentless attempts to posit fictions as *self-evident.* Throughout Modern Times, one of these fictions typically emerges as a *neutral center,* setting the scene for all the others. Reason, Money, Justice, Science, Man, Civilization, or Culture—with each there is the same phantasmagoric tendency: to posit the existence of a center, and then say that this center is ethically neutral. The State is thus the historical condition for the flourishing of these insipid terms.

33 Etymologically the modern State stems from the Indo-European root *st-*, which refers to fixity, to unchangeable things, to what *is*. More than a few have been fooled by this sleight of hand. Today, when the State does nothing more than outlive itself, the opposite becomes clear: it is civil war—*stasis* in Greek—that is permanence, and the modern State will have been a mere *reaction process* to this permanence.

GLOSS α: Contrary to what ONE would have us believe, the historicity specific to the fictions of "modernity" is never that of a stability gained once and for all, of a threshold finally surpassed, but precisely that of a process of *endless mobilization*. Behind the inaugural dates of the official historiography, behind the edifying epic tale of linear progress, a continuous labor of reorganization, of correction, of improvement, of papering over, of adjustment, and even sometimes of costly reconstruction has never stopped taking place. This labor and its repeated failures have given rise to the whole jittery junk heap of the "new." Modernity: not a stage where ONE comes to rest, but a task, an *imperative to modernize*, frenetically and from crisis to crisis, only to be finally overcome by our own fatigue and our own skepticism.

GLOSS β: "This state of affairs stems from a difference, which too often goes unnoticed, between modern societies and ancient societies, with regard to the notions of war and peace. The relation between the state of peace and the state of war has been, if one compares the past to the present, exactly reversed. For us peace is the normal state of affairs, which warfare happens to interrupt; for the ancients, warfare is normal, which peace happens to bring to an end."

—Émile Benveniste, *Le vocabulaire des institutions indo-européennes*

34 In both theory and practice, the modern State came into being in order to put an end to civil war, then called "wars of religion." Therefore, both historically and by its own admission, it is *secondary* vis-a-vis civil war.

GLOSS: Bodin's *The Six Books of the Commonwealth* [1576] was published four years after the St. Bartholomew's Day massacre, and Hobbes' *Leviathan* of 1651 eleven years after the start of the Long Parliament. The continuity of the modern State—from absolutism to the Welfare State—shall be that of an endlessly unfinished *war*, waged against civil war.

35 In the West, the unity of the traditional world was lost with the Reformation and the "wars of religion" that followed. The modern State then bursts on the scene with the task of reconstituting this unity—secularized, this time—no longer as an organic whole but instead as a *mechanical* whole, as a *machine*, as a conscious artificiality.

GLOSS α: What couldn't help but ruin all organicity of customary mediations during the Reformation was the gulf opened up by a doctrine professing the strict separation between faith and deed, between the kingdom of God and the kingdom of the world, between inner man and outer man. The religious wars thus present the absurd spectacle of a world that travels to the abyss just for having glimpsed it, of a harmony that breaks apart under the pressure of a thousand absolute and irreconcilable claims to wholeness. Indeed in this way, through sectarian rivalries, religions introduce the *idea* of ethical plurality despite themselves. But at this point civil war is still conceived by those who bring it about as something that will soon end, so that forms-of-life are not taken on but given over to *conversion* to this or that existing patron. Since that time the various uprisings of the Imaginary Party have taken it upon themselves to render obsolete Nietzsche's remark from 1882 that "the greatest progress of the masses up till now has been the religious war, for it proves that the mass has begun to treat concepts with respect."[7]

GLOSS β: Having run its historical course, the modern State rediscovers its old enemy: "sects." But this time it is not the State that is the ascendant political force.

36 The modern State put an end to the trouble that Protestantism first visited on the world by taking over its very mission. By *instituting* the fault between inner self and outer works identified by the Reformation, the modern State managed to extinguish the civil wars "of religion," and with them the religions themselves.

GLOSS: Henceforth there shall be on the one hand an "absolutely free," private, moral conscience and on the other hand public, political action "absolutely subject to State Reason." And these two spheres shall be distinct and independent. The modern State creates itself from nothing by extracting from the traditional ethical tissue the morally neutral space of political technique, sovereignty. Such creative gestures are those of a mournful marionette. The further away men have moved from this foundational moment, the more the meaning of the original act is lost. It is this same calm hopelessness that shines through in the classical maxim: *cuius regio, eius religio.*[8]

37 The modern State renders religions obsolete because it takes over for them at the bedside of the most atavistic phantasm of metaphysics: the One. From this point forward the order of the world will have to be ceaselessly restored and maintained at all costs, even as it constantly slips away from itself. Police and publicity[9] will be the purely fictive techniques that the modern State will employ to artificially maintain the fiction of the One. Its entire reality will be concentrated in these techniques, through which it will ensure the maintenance of Order, only now that of an outside order, a *public* order. And so all the arguments it advances in its own defense will in the end boil down to this: "Outside of me, disorder." Quite untrue: without it, *a multiplicity of orders*.

38 The modern State, which purports to put an end to civil war, is instead its continuation by other means.

GLOSS α: Is it necessary to read *Leviathan* to know that "because the major part hath by consenting voices declared a sovereign, he that dissented must now consent with the rest, that is, be contented to avow all the actions he shall do, or else justly be destroyed by the rest. [...] And whether he be of the congregation or not, and whether his consent be asked or not, he must either submit to their decrees or be left in the condition of war he was in before, wherein he might without injustice be destroyed by any man whatsoever."[10] The fate of the communards, of the Action Directe prisoners or the June 1848 insurgents tells us plenty about the bloody origins of republics. Herein lies the specific character of and obstacle to the modern State: it only persists through the practice of the very thing it wants to ward off, through the actualization of the very thing it claims to be absent. Cops know something about this, paradoxically having to *apply* a "state of law," which in fact depends on them alone. Thus was the destiny of the modern State: to arise first as the apparent victor of civil war, only then to be vanquished by it; to have been in the end only a parenthesis, only one party among others in the steady course of civil war.

GLOSS β: Wherever the modern State extended its reign, it exploited the same arguments, using similar formulations. These formulations are gathered together in their purest form and in their strictest logic in the writings of Hobbes. This is why all those who have wanted to confront the modern State have first had to grapple with this singular theoretician. Even today, at the height of the movement to liquidate the nation-state system, one hears open echoes of "Hobbesianism." Thus, as the French government finally aligned itself with a model of imperial decentralization during the convoluted affair of "Corsican autonomy," the government's Interior Minister resigned his position with the perfunctory pronouncement: "France does not need a new war of religion."

39 What at the molar scale assumes the aspect of the modern State, is called at the molecular scale the economic subject.

GLOSS α: We have reflected a great deal on the essence of the economy and more specifically on its "black magic" aspects.[11] The economy cannot be understood as a system of exchange, nor, therefore, as a relation between forms-of-life, unless it is grasped ethically: the economy as the production *of a certain type* of forms-of-life. The economy appears well prior to the institutions typically used to signal its emergence—the market, money, usury loans, division of labor—and it appears as a kind of *possession*, that is, as possession *by a psychic economy*. It is in this sense that the true black magic exists, and it is only at this level that the economy is real and concrete. This is also where its connection with the State is empirically observable. By flaring up like this the State ends up progressively creating economy in man, creating "Man" itself as an economic creature. With each improvement to the State the economy in each of its subjects is improved as well, and vice versa.

It would be easy to show how, over the course of the seventeenth century the nascent modern State imposed a monetary economy and everything that goes along with it in order to glean fuel for the rapid development of its machinery and its relentless military campaigns. Such work has already been performed elsewhere. But this approach only scratches the surface of the linkage between the State and the economy.

The modern State means, among other things, a progressively increasing monopoly on legitimate violence, a process whereby all other forms of violence are delegitimized. The modern State serves the general process of pacification which, since the end of the Middle Ages, only persists through its continuous intensification. It is not simply that during this evolution it always more drastically hinders the free play of forms-of-life, but rather that it works assiduously to break them, to tear them up, to extract bare life from them, an extraction that is the very activity of "civilization." In order to become a political subject in the modern State, *each body* must submit to the machinery that will make it such: it must begin by casting aside its passions (now inappropriate), its tastes (now laughable), its penchants (now contingent), endowing itself instead with *interests*, which are much more presentable and, even better, *representable*. In this way, in order to become a *political* subject each body must first carry out its own autocastration as an *economic* subject. Ideally, the political subject will thus be reduced to nothing more than a pure *vote*, a pure *voice*.

The essential function of the representation each society gives of itself is to influence the way in which each body is represented to itself, and through this to influence the structure of the psyche. The modern State is therefore first of all the constitution of *each body* into a molecular State, imbued with bodily integrity by way of territorial integrity, molded into a closed entity within a self, as much in opposition to the "exterior world" as to the tumultuous associations of its own penchants—which it must contain—and in the end required to comport itself with its peers as a good law-abiding subject, to be dealt with, along with other bodies, according to the universal proviso of a sort of private international law of "civilized" habits. In this way the more societies constitute themselves in States, the more their subjects embody the economy. They monitor themselves and each other, they control their emotions, their movements, their inclinations, and believe that they can expect the same self-control from others. They make sure never to get carried away where it might prove fatal, and stay cooped up in a room of their own where they can "let themselves go" at their leisure. Sheltered there, withdrawn within their frontiers, they calculate, they predict, they become a waypoint between past and future, and tie their fate to the most probable link between the two. That's it: they link up, put themselves in chains and chain themselves to each other, countering any type of excess. Fake self-control, restraint, self-regulation of the passions, extraction of a sphere of shame and fear—bare life—the warding off of all forms-of-life and *a fortiori* of any play established between them.

And so the dense and doleful intimidation of the modern State produces the economy, primitively and *existentially*, through a process that one could trace back to the twelfth century, and to the establishment of the first territorial courts. As Elias has pointed out exceedingly well, the most emblematic example of this *incorporation of the economy* was the induction of the warrior class into the society of the court, beginning with the twelfth-century codes of courtly conduct, then primers on *civility*, *prudence*, and *manners*, and finally with the rules of courtly etiquette at Versailles, the first substantial realization of a perfectly spectacular society in which all relations are mediated by images. As with all the forms of wild abandon on which medieval knighthood was founded, violence was slowly domesticated, that is, isolated as such, deprived of its ritual form, rendered illogical, and in the end cut down through mockery, through "ridicule," through the shame of fear and the fear of shame. Through the dissemination of this self-restraint, this *dread of getting carried away*, the State succeeded in creating the economic subject, in containing each being within its Self, that is, *within his body*, in *extracting bare life from each form-of-life*.

GLOSS β: "[T]he battlefield is, in a sense, moved within. Part of the tensions and passions that were earlier directly released in the struggle of man and man, must now be worked out within the human being. [...] [T]he drives, the passionate affects, that can no longer directly manifest themselves in the relationships *between* people, often struggle no less violently within the individual against this supervising part of themselves. And this semi-automatic struggle of the person with him or herself does not always find a happy resolution" (Norbert Elias, "State Formation and Civilization").[12]

As has been witnessed throughout "Modern Times," *the individual* produced by this process of economic embodiment carries within him a *crack*. And it is out of this crack that his bare life seeps. His acts themselves are full of cracks, broken from the inside. No self-abandon, no act of assumption can arise where the State's campaign of pacification—its war of *annihilation* directed against civil war—is unleashed. Here, instead of forms-of-life, we find an overproduction branching out in all directions, a nearly comical tree-like proliferation of *subjectivities*. At this point converges the double misfortune of the economy and the State: by caching civil war inside each person, the modern State put everyone at war against himself. This is where we begin.

40 The founding act of the modern State— that is, not the first act but the one it repeats over and over—is the institution of the fictitious split between public and private, between political and moral. This is how it manages to crack bodies open, how it grinds up forms-of-life. The move to divide internal freedom and external submission, moral interiority and political conduct, corresponds to the institution *as such* of bare life.

GLOSS: We know from experience the terms of the Hobbesian transaction between the subject and the sovereign: "I exchange my liberty for your protection. As compensation for my unwavering obedience, you must offer me safety." Safety, which is first posed as a way to shelter oneself from the prospect of death menaced by "others" takes on a whole new dimension during the course of *Leviathan*. From Chapter xxx: "by safety here is not meant a bare preservation, but also all other contentments of life, which every man by lawful industry, without danger or hurt to the commonwealth, shall acquire to himself."[13]

41 Depending on the side of the crack from which it is seen, the State's method of neutralization sets up two chimerical, distinct and interdependent monopolies: the monopoly of the political and the monopoly of critique.

GLOSS α: Certainly on the one hand the State claims to assume the *monopoly of the political*, of which the well-known expression "monopoly on legitimate violence" is merely the most vulgar indication. For the monopolization of the political requires the degradation of the differentiated unity of a world into a *nation*, then to degrade this nation into a *population* and a territory. It requires the disintegration of the entire organic unity of traditional societies in order to then submit the remaining fragments to a principle of *organization*. Finally, after having reduced society to a "pure indistinct mass, to a multitude decomposed into its atoms" (Hegel), the State assumes the role of artist giving form to these raw materials, and this according to the legible principle of the Law.[14]

On the other hand, the division between private and public gives rise to this second unreality, which matches the unreality of the State: critique. Of course it was Kant who crafted the general motto of critique in his *What is Enlightenment?* Oddly enough the motto was also a saying of Frederick II: "You are allowed to think as much as you want and on whatever topic you wish; as long as you obey!" Mirroring the political, "morally neutral" realm of State Reason, critique establishes the moral, "politically neutral" realm of free usage of Reason. This is what is meant by "publicity," first identified with the "Republic of Letters" but quickly appropriated as a State weapon against any rival ethical fabric, be it the unbreakable bonds of traditional society, the Cour des Miracles, or the language of the street. Thereafter another abstraction would respond to the State's abstract sphere of autonomous politics: the critical sphere of autonomous discourse. And just as the gestures of State reason had to be shrouded in silence, the idle chatter and the flights of fancy of critical reason will have to be shrouded in the condemnation of these gestures. Critique would therefore claim to be all the purer and more radical the more it alienated itself from any positive grounding for its own verbal fabrications. In exchange for renouncing all its directly political claims, that is, in abdicating all contestations of the State's monopoly on politics, critique will be granted a *monopoly on morality*. It will now have free reign to *protest*, as long as it does not pretend to exist in any other way. Gesture without discourse on the one hand and discourse without gesture on the other—the State and Critique guarantee by the techniques specific to each (police and publicity, respectively) the neutralization of every ethical difference. This is how THEY conjured away, along with the free play of forms-of-life, the political itself.

GLOSS β: After this it will come as little surprise that the most successful masterpieces of critique appeared exactly where "citizens" had been most fully deprived of access to the "political sphere," indeed, to the realm of practice as a whole; when all collective existence had been placed under the heel of the State, I mean: under the French and Prussian absolute monarchies of the eighteenth century. It should scarcely surprise us that the country of the State would also be the country of Critique, that France (for this is what we really mean) would be in every way, and even often avowedly, so perfectly at home in the eighteenth century. Given the contingency of our theater of operations, we are not averse to mentioning the constancy of a national character, which has been exhausted everywhere else. However, rather than show how, generation after generation, for more than two centuries, the State has produced critics and the critics have, in turn, produced the State, I think it more instructive to reproduce descriptions of pre-Revolutionary France made during the middle of the nineteenth century, that is, shortly after the events, by a mind at once detestable and quite shrewd:

"The government of the old regime had already taken away from the French any possibility, or desire, of helping one another. When the Revolution happened, one would have searched most of France in vain for ten men who had the habit of acting in common in an orderly way, and taking care of their own defense themselves; only the central power was supposed to take care of it."

"France [was] the European country where political life had been longest and most completely extinct, where individuals had most completely lost the practical skills, the ability to read facts, the experience of popular movements, and almost the very idea of the people."

"Since there no longer existed free institutions, and in consequence no political classes, no living political bodies, no organized political parties with leaders, and since in the absence of all these organized forces the direction of public opinion, when public opinion was reborn, devolved uniquely on the *philosophes*, it was to be expected that the Revolution be directed less by certain particular facts than by abstract principles and very general theories."

"The very situation of these writers prepared them to like general and abstract theories of government and to trust in them blindly. At the almost infinite distance from practice in which they lived, no experience tempered the ardors of their nature."

"We had, however, preserved one liberty from the destruction of all the others; we could philosophize almost without restraint on the origin of societies, on the essential nature of government, and on the primordial rights of the human species."

"All those injured by the daily practice of legislation soon took up this form of literary politics."

"Every public passion was thus wrapped up in philosophy; political life was violently driven back into literature."

And finally, at the end of the Revolution: "You will see an immense central power, which has devoured all the bits of authority and obedience which were formerly divided among a crowd of secondary powers, orders, classes, professions, families, and individuals, scattered throughout society."

— (Alexis de Tocqueville, *The Old Regime and the Revolution*, 1856)[15]

42 If certain theses such as "the war of each against each" are elevated to the level of governing principles, it is because they enable certain operations. So in this specific case we should ask: How can the "war of each against each" have begun before each person had been produced *as each*. And then we will see how the modern State presupposes the state of things that it produces; how it grounds the arbitrariness of its own demands in *anthropology*; how the "war of each against each" is instead the impoverished *ethic of civil war* imposed everywhere by the modern State under the name of the economic, which is nothing other than the universal reign of hostility.

GLOSS α: Hobbes used to joke about the circumstances of his birth, claiming it was induced after his mother had experienced a sudden fright: "Fear and I were born twins," as he put it.[16] But to my mind it makes more sense to attribute the wretchedness of the Hobbesian anthropology to excessive reading of that moron Thucydides than to his horoscope. So let us instead read the patter of our coward in a more appropriate light:

"The true and perspicuous explication of the Elements of Laws, Natural and Politic [...] dependeth upon the knowledge of what is human nature."

"The comparison of the life of man to a race [holdeth]. [...] But this race we must suppose to have no other goal, nor no other garland, but being foremost."

—Hobbes, *Human Nature*, 1640[17]

"Hereby it is manifest that during the time men live without a common power to keep them all in awe, they are in that condition which is called war, and such a war as is of every man against every man. For WAR consisteth not in battle only, or the act of fighting, but in a tract of time wherein the will to contend by battle is sufficiently known."

"Again, men have no pleasure, but on the contrary a great deal of grief, in keeping company where there is no power able to over-awe them all."

—Hobbes, *Leviathan*[18]

GLOSS β: Here Hobbes gives us the anthropology of the modern State, a positive albeit pessimistic anthropology, political albeit economic, that of an atomized city-dweller: "when going to sleep, he locks his doors," and "when even in his house, he locks his chests" (*Leviathan*).[19] Others have already shown how the State found it in its *political* interest to overturn, during the last few decades of the seventeenth century, the traditional ethics, to elevate *avarice*, the economic passion, from the rank of private vice to that of social virtue (cf. Albert O. Hirschmann). And just as this ethics, the ethics of equivalence, is the most worthless ethics that men have ever shared, the forms-of-life that correspond to it—the entrepreneur and the consumer—have distinguished themselves by a worthlessness that has become ever more pronounced with each passing century.

43 Rousseau thought he could confront Hobbes "on how the state of war springs from the social."[20] In so doing he proposed the Noble Savage in place of the Englishman's ignoble savage, one anthropology to replace another, only this time an optimistic one. But the mistake here was not the pessimism, it was the anthropology, and the desire to found a social order on it.

GLOSS α: Hobbes did not develop his anthropology merely by observing the problems of his age: the Fronde, the English Civil War, the nascent absolutist State in France, and the difference between them. Travelogues and other reports from New World explorers had been circulating for two centuries already. Less inclined to take on faith "that the condition of mere nature (that is to say, of absolute liberty, such as is theirs that neither are sovereigns nor subjects) is anarchy, and the condition of war," Hobbes attributed the civil war that he observed in "civilized" nations to a *relapse* into a state of nature that had to be averted using any means possible.[21] The savages of America and their state of nature, mentioned with horror in *De Cive* as well as in *Leviathan*, furnished a repulsive illustration: those beings who "(except the government of small families, the concord whereof dependeth on natural lust) have no government at all, and live at this day in [a] brutish manner" (*Leviathan*).[22]

GLOSS β: When one experiences thought in its barest form, the interval between a question and its answer can sometimes span centuries. Thus it was an anthropologist who, several months before killing himself, gave a response to Hobbes. The age, having reached the other side of the river of "Modern Times," found itself fully enmeshed in Empire. The text appeared in 1977 in the first issue of *Libre* under the title "Archeology of Violence." THEY tried to understand it, as well as the piece that follows, "Sorrows of the Savage Warrior," in isolation from the confrontation during the same decade that pitted the urban guerrilla against the old dilapidated structures of the bourgeois State, independently from the Red Army Faction, independently from the Red Brigades and the diffuse Autonomia movement.[23] And yet even with this craven reservation, the texts of Clastres still create a disturbance.

"What is primitive society? It is a multiplicity of undivided communities which all obey the same centrifugal logic. What institution at once expresses and guarantees the permanence of this logic? It is war, as the truth of relations between communities, as the principal sociological means of promoting the centrifugal force of dispersion against the centripetal force of unification. The war machine is the motor of the social machine; the primitive social being relies entirely on war, primitive society cannot survive without war. The more war there is, the less unification there is, and the best enemy of the State is war. Primitive society is society against the State in that it is society-for-war."

"Here we are once again brought back to the thought of Hobbes. [...] He was able to see that war and the State are contradictory terms, that they cannot exist together, that each implies the negation of the other: war prevents the State, the State prevents war. The enormous error, almost fatal amongst a man of this time, is to have believed that the society which persists in war of each against each is not truly a society; that the Savage world is not a social world; that, as a result, the institution of society involves the end of war, the appearance of the State, an anti-war machine par excellence. Incapable of thinking of the primitive world as a non-natural world, Hobbes nevertheless was the first to see that one cannot think of war without the State, that one must think of them in a relation of exclusion."[24]

44 The inability of the State's juridico-formal offensive to reduce civil war is not a marginal detail rooted in the fact that there is always a pleb to pacify, but appears centrally in the pacification procedure itself. Organizations modeled after the State characterize as "formless" that which within them derives in fact from the play of forms-of-life. In the modern State, this irreducibility is attested to by the infinite extension of the police, that is to say, of all that bears the inadmissable burden of realizing the conditions of possibility of a state order as vast as it is unworkable.

GLOSS α: Ever since the creation of the Paris Lieutenancy by Louis XIV, the practices of police institutions have continuously shown how the modern State has progressively *created its own society*. The police is that force that intervenes "wherever things are amiss," that is to say, wherever antagonism appears between forms-of-life—wherever there is a jump in *political* intensity. Using the arm of the police ostensibly to protect the "social fabric," while using another arm to destroy it, the State then offers itself as an existentially neutral mediator between the parties in question and imposes itself, even in its own coercive excesses, as the pacified landscape for confrontation. It is thus, according to the same old story, that the police *produced* public space as a space that it has taken control of; that is how the language of the State came to be applied to almost every social activity, how it became the *language of the social* par excellence.

GLOSS β: "The aim of oversight and provisions on the part of the police is to mediate between the individual [*Individuum*] and the universal possibility which is available for the attainment of individual ends. The police should provide for street-lighting, bridge-building, the pricing of daily necessities, and public health. Two main views are prevalent on this subject. One maintains that the police should have oversight over everything, and the other maintains that the police should have no say in such matters, since everyone will be guided in his actions by the needs of others. The individual [*der Einzelne*] must certainly have a right to earn his living in this way or that; but on the other hand, the public also has a right to expect that necessary tasks will be performed in the proper manner."[25]

   —Hegel, *Elements of the Philosophy of Right*
      (Addition to paragraph 236), 1833

45 At each moment of its existence, the police reminds the State of the violence, the banality, and the darkness of its beginnings.

46 The modern State fails in three ways: first, as the absolutist State, then as the liberal State, and soon after as the Welfare State. The passage from one to the other can only be understood in relation to three successive corresponding forms of civil war: the wars of religion, class struggle, and the Imaginary Party. It should be noted that the failure here is not in the result, but is the entire duration of the process itself.

GLOSS α: Once the first moment of violent pacification had passed, and the absolutist regime was established, the figure of the embodied sovereign lived on as the useless symbol of a bygone war. Rather than favoring pacification, the sovereign instead provoked confrontation, defiance, and revolt. It was clear that the taking on of this singular form-of-life—"such is my pleasure"[26]—came at the cost of repressing all the others. The liberal State corresponds to the surpassing of this aporia, the aporia of personal sovereignty, but only the surpassing of it *on its own ground*. The liberal State is a frugal State, which claims to exist only to ensure the free play of individual liberties, and to this end it begins by extorting interests from each body, so that it can attach them to these bodies and reign peacefully across this new abstract world: "the phenomenal republic of interests" (Foucault).[27] It claims it exists only to keep things in good order, for the proper functioning of "civil society," which is absolutely a thing of its own creation. Intriguingly, the glorious age of the liberal State, stretching from 1815 to 1914, would come to coincide with a multiplication of apparatuses of control, with the continuous monitoring and widespread disciplining of the population, and with society's complete submission to the police and publicity. "I have drawn attention to the fact that the development, dramatic rise, and dissemination throughout society of these famous disciplinary techniques for taking charge of the behavior of individuals day by day and in its fine detail is exactly contemporaneous with the age of freedoms"

(Foucault).[28] Security is the primary condition of "individual freedom" (which means nothing, because such a freedom must end where that of others begins). The State that "wishes to govern just enough so that it can govern the least" must in fact *know* everything, and it must develop a set of practices and technologies to do it. The police and publicity are the two agencies through which the liberal State gives transparency to the fundamental opacity of the population. Witness here the insidious way in which the liberal State will perfect the modern State, under the pretext of needing to penetrate everywhere in order to avoid being everywhere in actuality, that in order to leave its subjects alone it must know everything. The principle of the liberal State could be stated like this: "If control and discipline are everywhere, the State does not have to be so." "Government, initially limited to the function of supervision, is only to intervene when it sees that something is not happening according to the general mechanics of behavior, exchange, and economic life. [...] The Panopticon is the very formula of liberal government" (Foucault, *Birth of Biopolitics*).[29] "Civil society" is the name given by the liberal State for that which is both its own product and its own outside. It will not be surprising then to read that a study on French "values" concludes (without seeming to sense the contradiction) that in 1999 "the French are increasingly attached to personal freedom and public order" (*Le Monde*, November 16, 2000). Among the morons who respond to polls, that is, among those who still believe in *representation*, the majority are unhappy, emasculated lovers of the liberal State. In sum, "French civil society" only indicates the *proper functioning* of the set of disciplines and regimes of subjectivization *authorized* by the modern State.

GLOSS β: Imperialism and totalitarianism mark the two ways in which the modern State tried to leap beyond its own impossibility, first by slipping forward beyond its borders into colonial expansion, then by an intensive deepening of the penetration inside its own borders. In both cases, these desperate reactions from the State— which claimed to encompass *everything* just as it was becoming *nothing*—came to a head in the very forms of civil war the State claims *preceded it*.

47 Ultimately the "state-ification" of the social had to be paid for by the socialization of the State, and thus lead to the mutual dissolution of both the State and society. What THEY called the "Welfare State" was this indistinction (between society and state) in which the obsolete State-form survived for a little while within Empire. The incompatibility between the state order and its procedures (the police and publicity) expresses itself in the current efforts to dismantle the Welfare State. And so, on the same note, society no longer exists, at least in the sense of a differentiated whole. There is only a tangle of norms and mechanisms through which THEY hold together the scattered tatters of the global biopolitical fabric, through which THEY prevent its violent disintegration. Empire is the administrator of this desolation, the supreme manager of a process of listless implosion.

GLOSS α: There is an official history of the State in which the State seems to be the one and only actor, in which the advances of the state monopoly on the political are so many battles chalked up against an enemy who is invisible, imaginary, and precisely *without history*. And then there is a counter-history, written from the viewpoint of civil war, in which the stakes of all these "advancements," the *dynamics* of the modern State, can be glimpsed. This counter-history reveals a political monopoly that is constantly threatened by the recomposition of autonomous worlds, of non-state collectivities. Whenever the State left something to the "private" sphere, to "civil society," whenever it declared something to be insignificant, non-political, it left just enough room for the free play of forms-of-life such that, from one moment to the next, the monopoly on the political appears to be in dispute. This is how the State is led, either slowly or in a violent gesture, to encompass the totality of social activity, to take charge of the totality of man's existence. Thus, "the concept of the healthy individual in the service of the State was replaced by that of the State in the service of the healthy individual" (Foucault).[30] In France, this reversal was already established prior to the law of April 9, 1898 governing "Accident Liability—In Which the Victims Are Workers Practicing Their Profession" and *a fortiori* to the law of April 5, 1910 on retirement plans for peasants and laborers, which sanctioned *the right to life*. In taking the place, over the centuries, of all the heterogeneous mediations of traditional society, the State ended up with the opposite of its aim, and ultimately fell prey to its own impossibility. That which wanted to concentrate the monopoly of the political ended up politicizing everything; all aspects of life had become political, not in themselves as singular entities, but precisely insofar as the State, by taking a position, had there too formed itself into a *party*. Or how the State, in waging everywhere its war against civil war, above all propagated hostility toward itself.

GLOSS β: The Welfare State, which first took over for the liberal State within Empire, is the product of a massive diffusion of disciplines and regimes of subjectivation peculiar to the liberal State. It arises at the very moment when the concentration of these disciplines and these regimes—for example with the widespread practice of risk management—reaches such a degree in "society" that society is no longer distinguishable from the State. Man had thus become socialized to such an extent that the existence of a separate and personal State power becomes an obstacle to pacification. Blooms are no longer subjects—not economic subjects and even less legal subjects. They are creatures of imperial society. This is why they must first be taken on *as living beings* so that they may then continue existing fictitiously *as legal subjects.*

**Empire,
Citizen**

Therefore the sage takes his place over the people yet is no burden; takes his place ahead of the people yet causes no obstruction. That is why the empire supports him joyfully and never tires of doing so. It is because he does not contend that no one in the empire is in a position to contend with him.

— Lao Tzu, *Tao Te Ching*

48 The history of the modern State is the history of its struggle against its own impossibility—that is, the history of its being overwhelmed by the profusion of techniques it has deployed to ward off this impossibility. Empire is, to the contrary, the *assumption of both this impossibility* and these techniques. To be more exact, we will say that Empire is the *turning inside out* of the *liberal* State.

GLOSS α: We have, then, the official history of the modern State, namely the grand juridico-formal narrative of sovereignty: centralization, unification, rationalization. And also there is a counter-history, which is the history of its impossibility. You have to look into this other history—the growing mass of practices that must be adopted, the apparatuses put in place to keep up the fiction—to grasp a genealogy of Empire. In other words, the history of Empire does not take up where the modern State leaves off. Empire is what, at a certain point in time (let's say 1914), allows the modern State to live on *as a pure appearance*, as a lifeless form. The discontinuity here is not in the passage from one order to another, but cuts across time like two parallel but heterogeneous planes of consistency, just like the two histories of the State.

GLOSS β: When we speak of a turning inside out, we are referring to the final possibility of an exhausted system, which folds back onto itself in order, in a mechanical fashion, to collapse in on itself. The Outside becomes the Inside, and the Inside now has no limits. What was formerly *present* in a certain defined place now becomes *possible everywhere*. What is turned inside out no longer exists in a positive way, in a concentrated form, but remains in a suspended state as far as the eye can see. It is the final ruse of the system, the moment when it is most vulnerable and, at the same time, most impervious to attack. The operation whereby the liberal State is imperially folded back can be described as follows: The liberal State developed two sub-institutional practices that it used to control and keep at bay the population. On the one hand, there was the police in the original sense of the term ("The police keeps watch over the well-being of men [...] the police keeps watch over the living" [N. De La Mare, *Traité de la police*, 1705]) and, on the other hand, publicity, as a sphere equally accessible to all and therefore independent of every form-of-life. Each of these instances or agencies is in fact a set of practices and apparatuses with no real continuity other than their convergent effects on the population—the first on its "body," the second on its "soul." All that was needed to consolidate power was to control the social definition of happiness and to maintain order in the public sphere. These concerns allowed the liberal State to remain thrifty. Throughout the eighteenth and nineteenth centuries, the police and publicity developed in a way that both served and yet exceeded the institutions of the nation-state. It is only with World War I that they become the key nexus for how the liberal State is folded up into Empire. Then we witness something curious. By connecting them to each other in view of the war effort, and in a manner largely independent of national States, these sub-institutional practices give birth to the two super-institutional poles of Empire: the police becomes Biopower, and publicity is transformed into the Spectacle. From this point on, the State does not disappear, it is simply *demoted* beneath a transterritorial set of autonomous practices: Spectacle, Biopower.

GLOSS γ: The liberal hypothesis collapses in 1914, at the end of the "Hundred Years' Peace" that resulted from the Congress of Vienna. When the Bolshevik coup d'État occurred in 1917, each nation found itself torn in two by the global class struggle, and all illusions about an inter-national order had seen their day. In the global civil war, the process of polarization penetrates the frontiers of the State. If any order could still be glimpsed, it would have to be super-national.

GLOSS δ: If Empire is the assumption of the modern State's impossibility, it is also the assumption of the impossibility of imperialism. Decolonization was an important moment in the establishment of Empire, logically marked by the proliferation of puppet States. Decolonization means: the elaboration of new forms of horizontal, sub-institutional power that *function better* than the old ones.

49 The modern State's sovereignty was fictional and personal. Imperial sovereignty is pragmatic and impersonal. Unlike the modern State, Empire can legitimately claim to be democratic, insofar as it neither banishes nor privileges *a priori* any form-of-life.

And for good reason, since it is what assures the simultaneous attenuation of *all* forms-of-life, as well as their free play *within this attenuation*.

GLOSS α: Amidst the ruins of medieval society the modern State tried to reconstitute this unity around the principle of representation—that is, on the presumption that one part of society would be able to *incarnate* the totality of society. The term "incarnate" is not used here arbitrarily. The doctrine of the modern State *explicitly* secularizes one of the most fearsome operations of Christian theology: the one whose dogma is expressed by the Nicene Creed. Hobbes devotes a chapter to it in the appendix of *Leviathan*. His theory of personal sovereignty is based on the doctrine that makes the Father, Son and Holy Ghost the three *persons* of God, "meaning that each can play its own role but also that of the others." This makes it possible for the Sovereign to be defined as an actor on behalf of those who have decided to "appoint one man or assembly of men to bear their person" and thus "every one to own and acknowledge himself to be author of whatsoever he that so beareth their person shall act, or cause to be acted, in those things which concern the common peace and safety, and therein to submit their wills" (*Leviathan*).[31] If, in the iconophilic theology of Nicea, Christ or the icon manifests not the presence of God but his essential absence, his sensible withdrawal, his unrepresentability, then for the modern State the personal sovereign manifests the *fictive* withdrawal of "civil society." The modern State is conceived therefore as a part of society that takes no part in society, and can for this reason represent it as a whole.

GLOSS β: The various bourgeois revolutions never tampered with the principle of personal sovereignty, insofar as an assembly or leader, elected directly or indirectly, never deviated from the idea of a possible representation of the social totality, i.e. of society *as a totality*. As a result, the passage from the absolutist State to the liberal State only managed to liquidate the one person—the King—who liquidated the medieval order from which he emerged, and whose last living vestige he seemed to be. It is only as an obstacle to his own historical processes that the king was judged: he composed his own sentence, his death the period at the end of it. Only the democratic principle, promoted from within by the modern State, was able finally to bring down the modern State. The democratic idea— the absolute equivalence of all forms-of-life—is also an imperial idea. Democracy is imperial to the extent that the equivalence among forms-of-life can only be implemented *negatively*, by preventing, with all the means at its disposal, ethical differences from attaining in their play an intensity that makes them political. This would introduce lines of rupture, alliances and discontinuities into the smooth space of demokratic society that would ruin the equivalence of forms-of-life. This is why Empire and demokracy are nothing, positively, other than the free play of attenuated forms-of-life, as when one speaks of an attenuated virus that is used as a vaccine. In one of his only texts on the State, the *Critique of Hegel's "Philosophy of Right,"* Marx in this way defended the imperial perspective of the "material State," which he opposed to the "political State," in the following terms:

"The *political* republic is democracy within the abstract form of the state. Hence the abstract state-form of democracy is the republic."

"*Political life* in the modern sense is the *Scholasticism* of popular life. *Monarchy* is the fullest expression of this estrangement. The *republic* is the negation of this estrangement within its own sphere."

"[A]ll forms of the state have democracy *for* their truth, and for that reason are false to the extent that they are not democracy."

"In true democracy *the political state disappears*."[32]

GLOSS γ: Empire can only be understood through the *biopolitical* turn of power. Like Biopower, Empire does not correspond to any positive juridical framework, and is not a new institutional order. It instead designates a *reabsorption* or retraction of the old substantial sovereignty. Power has always circulated in microphysical, familiar, everyday, material and linguistic apparatuses. It has always cut across the life and bodies of subjects. What is novel about Biopower is that *it is nothing more than this*. Biopower is a form of power that no longer rises up over against "civil society" as a sovereign hypostasis, as a Great Exterior Subject. It can no longer be *isolated* from society. Biopower means only that power adheres to life and life to power. Thus, from the perspective of its classical form, power is changing radically before our eyes, from a solid to a gaseous, molecular state. To coin a formula: *Biopower is the SUBLIMATION of power.* Empire cannot be conceived outside of this understanding of our age. Empire is not and cannot be a power separated from society. Society won't stand for that, just as it crushes the final remnants of classical politics with its indifference. Empire is immanent to "society." It is "society" *insofar as society is a power.*

50 Empire exists "positively" only in crisis, only as negation and reaction. If we too belong to Empire, it is only because it is impossible to get outside it.

GLOSS α: The imperial regime of pan-inclusion always follows the same plot: something, for whatever reason, manifests its foreignness to Empire, or shows itself trying to escape from it, trying to have done with it. This state of affairs constitutes a crisis, and Empire responds with a *state of emergency*. It is at this passing moment, during one of these reactive operations, that ONE can say: "Empire exists."

GLOSS β: It is not that imperial society represents an achievement, a plenitude without remainder. The space left free by the deposing of personal sovereignty remains just that, empty vis-à-vis society. This space, the place of the Prince, is currently occupied by the Nothing of an imperial *Principle* that materializes and comes into focus only when it strikes like lightning at anything pretending to remain outside of it. This is why Empire is not only without a government, but also without an emperor: there are only *acts of government*, all equally *negative*. In our historical experience, the phenomenon that comes closest to this state of affairs is still the Terror. Where "universal freedom … can produce neither a positive work nor a deed; there is left for it only *negative* action; it is merely the *fury* of destruction" (Hegel, *Phenomenology of Spirit*, 359).

GLOSS γ: Empire functions best when crisis is ubiquitous. Crisis is Empire's regular mode of existence, in the same way that an insurance company comes into being only when there's an accident. The temporality of Empire is the temporality of emergency and catastrophe.

51 Empire is not the crowning achievement of a civilization, the end-point of its ascendent arc. Rather it is the tail-end of an inward turning process of disaggregation, as that which must check and if possible arrest the process. Empire is therefore the kat-echon. "'Empire' in this sense meant the historical power to restrain the appearance of the Antichrist and the end of the present eon" (Carl Schmitt, *The Nomos of the Earth*, 59–60). Empire sees itself as the final bulwark against the eruption of chaos, and acts with this minimal perspective in mind.

52 At first glance, Empire seems to be a parodic recollection of the entire, frozen history of a "civilization." And this impression has a certain intuitive correctness. Empire is in fact civilization's last stop before it reaches the end of its line, the final agony in which it sees its life pass before its eyes.

53 With the liberal State being turned inside out into Empire, ONE has passed from a world partitioned by the Law to a space polarized by norms. The Imaginary Party is the *other, hidden side* of this turning inside out.

GLOSS α: What do we mean by Imaginary Party? *That the Outside has moved inside.* This turning inside out happened noiselessly, peacefully, like a thief in the night. At first glance, it seems nothing has changed. ONE is simply struck by the sudden futility of so many familiar things, and the old divisions that can no longer account for what is happening are now suddenly so burdensome.

Some nagging little neurosis makes ONE still want to distinguish just from unjust, healthy from sick, work from leisure, criminal from the innocent and the ordinary from the monstrous. But let's admit the obvious: these old divisions no longer have any meaning.

It is not as if they have been suppressed, though. They are still there, but they are *inconsequential.* The norm hasn't abolished the Law, it has merely voided the Law and commandeered it for its own purposes, putting it in the service of its own immanent practices of calculation and administration. When the Law enters the force-field of the norm, it loses the last vestiges of transcendence, from now on functioning only in a kind of indefinitely renewed state of exception.

The state of exception is the *normal* regime of the Law.

There is no visible Outside any more—nothing like *a* pure Nature, *the* Madness of the classical age, *the* Great Crime of the classical age, or *the* Great *classical* Proletariat with its actually-existing Homeland of Justice and Liberty. These are all gone, mostly because they have lost their imaginary force of attraction. The Outside is now gone precisely because today there is exterior*ity* at every point of the biopolitical tissue.

Madness, crime or the hungry proletariat no longer inhabit a defined or recognized space, they no longer form a world unto themselves, their own ghetto with or without walls. With the dissipation of the social, these terms become reversible modalities, a violent latency, a possibility *each and every body* might be capable of. This suspicion is what justifies the continuous socialization of society, the perfecting of the micro-apparatuses of control. Not that Biopower claims to govern men and things directly—instead, it governs *possibilities* and *conditions* of possibility.

Everything that had its source in the Outside— illegality, first of all, but also misery and death—is *administered* and therefore taken up in an *integration* that *positively* eliminates these exteriorities in order to allow them to recirculate. This is why there is no such thing as death within Biopower: there is *only murder* and its circulation. Through statistics, an entire network of causalities embeds each living being in the collection of deaths his own survival requires (the dropouts, the unfortunate Indonesians, workplace accidents, Ethiopians of all ages, celebrities killed in car crashes, etc.). But it is also in a *medical* sense that death has become murder, with the proliferation of "brain dead corpses," these "living dead" who would have passed away a long time ago if they weren't kept alive artificially as organ banks for some absurd transplant, if they weren't being kept alive in order *to be passed away*. The truth is that now there is no outside that can be identified as such, since the threshold itself has become *the intimate condition of all that exists*.

The Law sets up divisions and institutes distinctions, it circumscribes what defies it and recognizes an orderly world to which it gives both form and duration. The Law ceaselessly names and enumerates what it outlaws. The Law *says its outside*. The inaugural gesture of the Law is to exclude, and first of all its own foundation: sovereignty, violence. But the norm has no sense of foundation. It has no memory, staying as close as possible to the present, always claiming to be on the side of immanence. While the Law gives a face and honors the sovereignty of what is outside it, the norm is acephalous—headless—and is delighted every time a king's head gets cut off. The norm has no *hieros*, no place of its own, acting invisibly over the entirety of the gridded, edgeless space it distributes. No one is excluded here or expelled into some identifiable outside. What is called "excluded" is, for the norm, just a modality of a generalized inclusion. It is therefore no longer anything but a single, solitary field, homogenous but diffracted into an infinity of nuances, a regime of limitless integration that sets out to maintain the play between forms-of-life at the lowest possible level of intensity. In this space, an ungraspable agency of totalization reigns, dissolving, digesting, absorbing and deactivating all alterity a priori. A process of omnivorous immanentization—reducing everything to nothing—deploys itself on a planetary scale. The goal: *make the world into continuous biopolitical tissue.* And all this time, the norm stands watch.

Under the regime of the norm, nothing is normal, but everything must be *normalized*. What functions here is a *positive* paradigm of power. The norm produces all that is, insofar as the norm is itself, as ONE says, the *ens realissimum*. Whatever does not belong to its mode of unveiling is not, and whatever is not cannot belong to its mode of unveiling. Under the regime of the norm, negativity is never recognized as such, but reduced to a simple *default* in relation to the norm, a *hole* to mend into the global biopolitical tissue. Negativity, this power that is not *supposed* to exist, is thus logically abandoned to a traceless disappearance. Not without reason, since the Imaginary Party is the Outside of the world without Outside, the essential discontinuity lodged at the heart of a world rendered continuous.

The Imaginary Party is the *seat*, and the *siege*, of potentiality.

GLOSS β: There is no better illustration of how the norm has subsumed the Law than to consider how the old territorial States of Europe "abolished" their borders after the Schengen Agreement. This abolition of borders, which is to say the abandonment of the most sacred aspect of the modern State, does not mean of course that the States themselves will disappear, but rather it signals the permanent possibility of their restoration, if the circumstances demand it. In this sense, when borders are abolished, customs checkpoints in no way disappear but are extended to virtually all places and times. Under Empire borders come to resemble what are called "mobile" customs checkpoints, which can be placed, impromptu, at any point within a territory.

54 Empire has never had any juridical or institutional existence, *because it needs none.* Unlike the modern State, which pretended to be an order of Law and of Institutions, Empire is the *guarantor* of a reticular proliferation of norms and apparatuses. Under normal circumstances, Empire *is* these apparatuses.

GLOSS α: Every time Empire intervenes, it leaves behind norms and apparatuses that allow the crisis site to be *managed* as a transparent space of circulation. This is how imperial society makes itself known: as an immense articulation of apparatuses that pump an electrical life into the fundamental inertia of the biopolitical tissue. Because the reticular gridwork of imperial society is always threatened with breakdowns, accidents and blockages, Empire makes sure to eliminate resistances to circulation, liquidating all obstacles to penetration, making everything transparent to social flows. Empire is also what secures transactions and guarantees what might be called a *social superconductivity*. This is why Empire has no center: it makes it possible for each node of its network to be a center. All we can ever make out along the global assemblage of local apparatuses are the condensations of forces and the deployment of *negative operations* that ensure the progress of imperial transparency. Spectacle and Biopower assure not just the intensive continuity of flows, but the transitive normalization—their being made equivalent—of all situations as well.

GLOSS β: There are no doubt "overwhelmed" zones where imperial control is denser than elsewhere, where each small segment of what exists pays its due to the general panopticism, and where at a certain point the population can no longer be distinguished from the police. Inversely, there are also zones where Empire seems absent and lets everyone know it "doesn't dare set foot there." This is because it *calculates*, weighs, evaluates and then *decides* to be here or there, to show up or withdraw, all for tactical reasons. Empire is not everywhere, and nowhere is it absent. Unlike the modern State, Empire has no interest in being the summit, in being the always visible and resplendent sovereign. Empire only claims to be the *last resort* in each situation. Just as there is nothing natural about a "nature park" created by the administrators of artificialization who have *decided* it is preferable to leave it "intact," so too Empire is present even when it is effectively absent, present as withdrawn. Empire is such that it *can* be everywhere. It resides in each point of the territory, in the gap between normal and exceptional situations. Empire has the *power* to be weak.

GLOSS γ: The logic of the modern State is a logic of the Law and the Institution. Institutions and the Law are deterritorialized and, in principle, abstract. In this way, they distinguish themselves from the customs they replace, customs which are always local, ethically permeated, and always open to existential contestation. Institutions and the Law loom over men, their permanence drawn from their transcendence, from their own inhuman self-assertion. Institutions, like the Law, establish lines of partition and give names in order to separate and put things in order, putting an end to the chaos of the world, or rather corralling chaos into the delimited space of the *unauthorized*— Crime, Madness, Rebellion. And both Law and

Institutions are united in the fact that neit
need to justify itself to anyone, no matter v
Law is the Law," says the man.

Even if it does not mind using them as *w*
it does with everything else, Empire knows
about the abstract logic of the Law and the Inst
Empire knows only *norms* and *apparatuses*. Like
ratuses, norms are local. They take effect in th
and now insofar as they *function*, empirically. N
hide neither their origin nor their reason for existir
these are to be found outside the norms themselves
the conflicts which give rise to them. What is essent
today is not some preliminary declaration of universali
that would then strive to enforce itself. Attention mus
be paid to *operations*, to the pragmatic. There is indeed
a totalization here as well, but it does not emerge out
of a desire for universalization. It takes place through
the *articulation* of apparatuses, through the continuity
of the circulation between them.

GLOSS δ: Under Empire we witness a proliferation of
the legal, a chronic boom in juridical production. This
proliferation, far from confirming some sort of triumph of the Law, instead verifies its total devaluation,
its definitive obsolescence. Under the regime of the
norm, the Law becomes but one instrument among
many for retroactively acting on society, an instrument
that can be as easily customized—and subject to reversal
of sense—as all the others. It is a *technique of government*, a way of putting an end to a crisis, nothing more.

What the modern State elevated to the sole source of right—the Law—is now nothing more than one of the expressions of the social norm. Even judges no longer have the subordinate task of qualifying facts and applying the Law, but the sovereign function of evaluating the opportunity such and such a judgment affords. The vagueness of laws, which increasingly have recourse to the nebulous criteria of normality, are no longer seen as hindering the laws' effectiveness; to the contrary, this vagueness becomes a condition for the survival of these laws and for their applicability to any and every case that might come before them. When judges "legislate from the bench" and the social is increasingly juridicized, they are doing nothing other than ruling in the name of the norm. Under Empire, an "anti-mafia" trial does nothing but celebrate the triumph of one mafia—the judges—over another—the judged. Here, the sphere of Law has become one weapon among others in the universal deployment of hostility. If Blooms can only connect and torture one another in the legal terms, Empire by contrast doesn't take well to this same language, nevertheless making use of it from time to time when the opportunity is right; and even then it continues to speak the only language it knows, the language of *effectiveness*, of the effective capacity to *re-establish the normal situation*, to produce public order, the smooth general functioning of the Machine. Two increasingly similar figures of this sovereignty of effectiveness make their presence felt thus in the very convergence of their functions: the *cop* and the *doctor*.

GLOSS ε: "The law should be used as just another weapon in the government's arsenal, and in this case it becomes little more than a propaganda cover for the disposal of unwanted members of the public. For this to happen efficiently, the activities of the legal services have to be tied into the war effort in as discreet a way as possible."

—Frank Kitson, *Low Intensity Operations: Subversion, Insurgency, Peace-Keeping* (1971).

55 "Citizen" is anything that shows some degree of ethical neutralization, some attenuation that is compatible with Empire. *Difference* is not done away with completely, as long as it is expressed against the backdrop of a general equivalence. Indeed, difference is the elementary unit used in the imperial management of identities. If the modern State reigned over the "phenomenal republic of interests,"[33] Empire can be said to reign over the *phenomenal republic of differences*. It is through this depressing masquerade that all expressions of forms-of-life get conjured away. Imperial power stays impersonal because it has the power that personalizes. Imperial power totalizes because it is itself what individuates. We are dealing not so much with individualities and subjectivities, but with individuations and subjectivations—transitory, disposable, modular. *Empire is the free play of simulacra.*

GLOSS α: Empire's unity is not imposed on reality as an extra, supplementary form. It comes about at the lowest level, on a molecular scale. The unity of Empire is nothing other than the global uniformity of attenuated forms-of-life produced through the conjunction of Spectacle and Biopower. Its unity is more a moiré pattern than multicolored: made up of differences, but only *in relation to the norm*. Normalized differences. Statistical deviations. Under Empire, nothing forbids you from being a little bit punk, slightly cynical, or moderately S & M. Empire tolerates all transgressions, provided they remain *soft*. We are no longer dealing with a voluntaristic a priori totalization, but with molecular calibrations of subjectivities and bodies. "[A]s power becomes more anonymous and more functional, those on whom it is exercised tend to be more strongly individualized" (Foucault, *Discipline and Punish*).[34]

GLOSS β: "And the whole inhabited world, as it were attending a national festival, has laid aside its old dress, the carrying of weapons, and has turned, with full authority to do so, to adornments and all kinds of pleasures. And all the other sources of contention have died out in the cities, but this single rivalry holds all of them, how each will appear as fair and charming as possible. Everything is full of gymnasiums, fountains, gateways, temples, handicrafts, and schools. And it can be said in medical terms that the inhabited world was, as it were, ill at the start and has now recovered. [...] the whole earth has been adorned like a pleasure garden.

Gone beyond land and sea is the smoke rising from the fields and the signal fires of friend and foe, as if a breeze had fanned them away. There has been introduced instead every kind of charming spectacle and a boundless number of games. [...] Therefore those outside your empire, if there are any, alone should be pitied since they are deprived of such advantages."

—Aelius Aristedes, "Regarding Rome," 144 CE

56 From here on out, citizen will mean: citizen of Empire.

GLOSS: In the Roman empire, citizenship was not limited to Romans. It was open to anyone who, in each province of the Empire, demonstrated a sufficient ethical conformity with the Roman model. Citizenship, in its juridical sense, merely corresponded to someone's own labor of self-neutralization. As you can see, the term "citizen" does not belong to the language of the Law, but to that of the norm. All appeals to the citizen are, and have been since the French Revolution, emergency measures: a practice that corresponds with a state of exception ("the Homeland is in danger," "the Republic is threatened," etc.). The appeal to the citizen is therefore never an appeal to a legal subject, but an injunction imposed on the legal subject to go beyond itself and give up its life, to behave in an exemplary fashion, and *to be more than a legal subject in order to remain one.*

57 The only thought compatible with Empire—when it is not sanctioned as its official thought—is deconstruction. Those who celebrated it as "weak thought" were right on target. Deconstruction is a discursive practice guided by one unique goal: *to dissolve and disqualify all intensity, while never producing any itself.*

GLOSS: Nietzsche, Artaud, Schmitt, Hegel, Saint Paul, German romanticism, and surrealism: deconstruction's task is, apparently, to produce fastidious commentaries targeting anything that, in the history of thought, has carried any intense charge. This new form of policing that pretends to be a simple extension of literary criticism beyond its date of expiration is, in fact, quite effective in its own domain. It won't be long before it has managed to rope off and quarantine everything from the past that is still a little virulent within a *cordon sanitaire* of digressions, reservations, language games and winks, using its tedious tomes to prevent the prolongation of thought into gesture—in short, to struggle tooth and nail against the event. No surprise that this wave of global prattle emerged out of a critique of metaphysics understood as privileging the "simple and immediate" presence of speech over writing, of life over the text and its multiplicity of significations. It would certainly be possible to interpret deconstruction as a simple Bloomesque reaction. The deconstructionist, incapable of having an effect on even the smallest detail of his world, being literally *almost no longer in the world* and having made absence his permanent mode of being, tries to embrace his Bloomhood with bravado. He shuts himself up in that narrow, closed circle of realities that still affect him at all—books, texts, films, and music— because these things are as insubstantial as he is. He can no longer see anything in what he reads that might relate to life, and instead sees what he lives as a tissue of references to what he has already read. Presence and the world as a whole, insofar as Empire allows, are for him purely hypothetical. Reality and experience are for him nothing more than dubious appeals to authority. There is something *militant* about deconstruction, a militancy of absence, an offensive retreat into the closed but indefinitely recombinable world of significations. Indeed, beneath an appearance of complacency, deconstruction has a very specific political function. It tries to pass off anything that violently opposes Empire as *barbaric*, it deems *mystical* anyone who takes his own presence to self as a source of energy for his revolt, and makes anyone who follows the vitality of thought with a *gesture* a *fascist*. For these sectarian agents of preventive counter-revolution, the only thing that matters is the extension of the epochal suspension that fuels them. Immediacy, as Hegel has already explained, is the most abstract determination. And our deconstructionists know well that the *future of Hegel is Empire*.

58 Empire perceives civil war neither as an affront to its majesty nor as a challenge to its omnipotence, but simply as a *risk*. This explains the preventive counter-revolution that Empire continues to wage against anyone who might puncture *holes* in the biopolitical continuum. Unlike the modern State, Empire does not deny the existence of civil war. Instead, it *manages* it. By admitting the existence of civil war, Empire furnishes itself with certain convenient means to steer or contain it. Wherever its networks are insufficiently intrusive, it will ally itself for as long as it takes with some local mafia or even a local guerilla group, on the condition that these parties guarantee they will maintain order in the territory they have been assigned. Nothing matters less to Empire than the question, "who controls what?"—provided, of course, that *control has been established*. As a result, *not reacting is, in this way, still a reaction.*

GLOSS α: It is amusing to see the absurd contortions Empire's incursions require of those who want to oppose Empire but are skittish of outright civil war. The imperial operation in Kosovo was not directed against the Serbs but against civil war itself, having become all too visible in the Balkans. And so the good souls of the world, compelled to *take a position*, were forced to side with either NATO or Milosevic.

GLOSS β: On the heels of Genoa and its scenes of Chilean-style repression, a high-ranking official of the Italian police offered this touching admission to *La Repubblica*: "Look, I'm going to tell you something that's not easy for me and that I have never told anyone. [...] The police aren't there to put things in order, but to govern disorder."

59 Ideally, the cybernetic reduction would posit Bloom as a transparent conductor of social information. Empire would gladly represent itself, then, as a *network* in which everyone would be a *node*. In each of these nodes, the norm makes up the element of social conductivity. Even before the circulation of information, a *biopolitical causality* passes through it with more or less resistance, depending upon the gradient of normality. Each node—country, body, firm, political party—is held *responsible* for its resistance. This is even the case to the point of the absolute non-conductivity, to the point of the refraction of flows. The node in question will then be declared guilty, criminal, inhuman, and will become the object of an imperial intervention.

GLOSS α: Because no one is ever depersonalized enough to be a perfect conductor of these social flows, everyone is always-already, as the very condition of survival, *at fault* in the eyes of the norm, a norm that will only be established after the fact, after the intervention. We call this state a *blank blame*.[35] It is the moral condition of the citizen of Empire. It is the reason why there are, in fact, no citizens, but only *proofs* of citizenship.

GLOSS β: The network's informality, plasticity, and opportunistic incompleteness offer a model of weak solidarity from whose loose bonds imperial "society" is woven.

GLOSS γ: What is finally made clear by the planetary circulation of responsibility—when the world is cross-examined to the point where even "natural disasters" are perpetrated by some guilty party—is how all causality is essentially *constructed*.

GLOSS δ: Empire has the habit of launching "public awareness campaigns." These amount to a deliberate heightening of the sensitivity of those social sensors alert to this or that phenomenon—that is, in the creation of this phenomenon as a phenomenon, and in the construction of the causal chains that allow for its materialization.

60 The jurisdiction of the imperial police, of Biopower is limitless, since what it must circumscribe and put a stop to does not exist at the level of the actual *but at the level of the possible*. The discretionary power here is called *prevention* and the risk factor is *this possible, existing everywhere in actuality as possible*, which is the basis for Empire's universal right to intervene.

GLOSS α: The enemy of Empire is within. The enemy is the event. It is everything that *might* happen, everything that might disturb the mesh of norms and apparatuses. Logically therefore the enemy, in the form of *risk*, is omnipresent. And concern is the only *acknowledged* reason for the brutal imperial interventions against the Imaginary Party: "Look how ready we are to protect you, since as soon as something exceptional happens— obviously without taking into account quaint customs like law or jurisprudence—we are going to intervene using any means necessary" (Foucault).

GLOSS β: There is obviously a certain Ubuesque quality to imperial power, which paradoxically seems ill-fit to undermine the effectiveness of the Machine. In the same way, there is a *baroque* aspect to the juridical framework under which we live. In fact, it seems vital to Empire that it maintain a certain amount of permanent confusion around enforced rules, rights, and the various authorities and their competencies. It is this confusion that enables Empire to deploy, when the time comes, *any means necessary*.

61 It is no use distinguishing between cops and citizens. Under Empire, the difference between the police and the population is abolished. At any moment each citizen of Empire can, through a characteristically Bloomesque reversal, reveal himself a cop.

GLOSS α: Foucault dates back to the second half of the eighteenth century the origin of the idea that "the delinquent is the enemy of society as a whole." Under Empire, this notion extends to the totality of the reconstructed social cadaver. Both for himself and for others, and in virtue of his status as blank blame, each person is a risk, a potential hostis. This kind of schizoid situation explains the revival, under Empire, of mutual monitoring and informing, of policing both within and among citizens. For it is not only that the citizens of Empire denounce anything that seems "abnormal" to them with such fervor that even the police can no longer keep up, it is that they sometimes denounce themselves in order to have done with the blank blame they feel, so that their still unresolved status, and the uncertainty as to their membership within the biopolitical tissue, might be cleared up with the fell swoop of judgment. And it is through this mechanism of generalized terror that all risky dividuals are everywhere pushed out, quarantined, spontaneously isolated—all those who, being subject to imperial intervention, could bring down with them, through capillary action, the adjoining links in the network.

GLOSS β:
"—How would you define the police?
The police come from the public and the public forms a part of the police. Those on the police force are paid to devote all their time to carrying out their duties, but these duties are equally those of all their fellow citizens.

—What is the primary role of the police?

They have an expanded mission, focused on the resolution of problems, what is known as 'problem-solving policing.'

—How do you measure the effectiveness of the police?

The lack of crime and lawlessness.

—What specifically do the police take care of?

The problems and concerns of the citizens.

—What determines the effectiveness of the police?

The cooperation of the public.

—How do you define professionalism in a police force?

An ability to remain in contact with the population in order to anticipate problems.

—What opinion do the police have of judicial proceedings?

They are one means among many."

—Jean-Paul Brodeur, Professor of Criminology, Montréal. Quoted in *Guide pratique de la police de proximité* [*Practical Guide to Community Policing*], Paris, March 2000.

62 Imperial sovereignty means that no point of space or time and no element of the biopolitical tissue is safe from intervention. The electronic archiving of the world, generalized traceability, the fact that the means of production are becoming just as much a means of control, the reduction of the juridical edifice to a mere weapon in the arsenal of the norm—all this tends to turn everyone into *a suspect*.

GLOSS: A portable phone becomes a black box, a mode of payment a record of your buying habits, your parents turn into snitches, a telephone bill becomes a file on your acquaintances: the whole overproduction of useless personal information ends up being critically important simply because at any moment it is *usable*. This *available* is what bathes every gesture in the shadow of threat. That Empire leaves this information relatively unexploited indicates precisely its own sense of security, how little, for now, it feels threatened.

63 Empire is scarcely thought, and perhaps hardly thinkable, within the western tradition, that is, within the limits of the metaphysics of subjectivity. The best THEY have been able to do is to think the surpassing of the modern State on its own grounds. This has spawned a number of unsustainable projects for a universal State, whether in the form of the speculations on cosmopolitan right that would establish perpetual peace, or as the ridiculous hope for a global democratic state, which is the ultimate goal of Negriism.

GLOSS α: Those who cannot manage to imagine the world except through the categories allotted to them by the liberal State, commonly pretend to confuse Empire, here denounced as "globalization," with one or another super-national organization (the IMF, the World Bank, the WTO or the UN, or less often NATO and the European Commission). From counter-summit to counter-summit, we see our "anti-globalization" movement consumed more and more by doubt: What if inside these pompous edifices, behind these proud facades, there was NOTHING? Intuitively they realize that these grand global shells are empty, and this is, moreover, why they besiege them. These palace walls are made from nothing but good intentions. They were constructed each in their time as a *reaction* to some world crisis, and since then have been left there, uninhabited, unusable for anything, to serve, for example, as a decoy for the dissenting herds of Negriism.

GLOSS β: It is hard to understand what someone is driving at when, after a lifetime of disavowals, he asserts in an article titled "'Empire,' The Ultimate Stage of Imperialism"[36] that "in the current imperial phase, there is no more imperialism," or when he proclaims that the dialectic is dead and that we must "theorize and act both *within* and *against* Empire at the same time": someone who takes by turns the masochist's position of demanding that these institutions dissolve themselves and that of imploring them to exist. And so, one should not begin with his writings, but with what he has actually done.

Even when it comes to understanding a book like *Empire*—a certain variety of theoretical mishmash that achieves in thought the same ultimate reconciliation of all incompatibilities that Empire dreams of realizing in deeds—it is more instructive to observe the practices that claim to represent it. In this way, in the discourse of the spectacular bureaucrats of the White Overalls, the phrase "people of Seattle" has been replaced, for some time now, with "multitude." "The *people*," Hobbes reminds us, "is somewhat that is *one*, having *one will*, and to whom *one action* may be attributed; none of these can properly be said of a multitude. The *people* rules in all governments. For even in *monarchies* the *people* commands; for the *people* wills by the will of *one man*; but the multitude are citizens, that is to say, subjects. In a *democracy* and *aristocracy*, the citizens are the *multitude*, but the *court* is the *people*."[37] The entire Negrian perspective boils down to this: to force Empire to take on the form of a universal State, by staging the emergence of a so-called "global civil society." Coming from people *who have always aspired to hold institutional positions*, who thus *have always pretended to believe in the fiction of the modern State*, the absurdity of this strategy becomes clear; and the evidence to the contrary in *Empire* itself acquires historical significance. When Negri asserts that the multitude produced Empire, that "sovereignty has taken a new form, composed of national and supranational organisms united under a single logic of rule," that "Empire is the political subject that effectively regulates these global exchanges, the sovereign power that governs the world," or again that "[t]his order is expressed as a juridical formation," he gives an account, not of the world around him, but of his own ambitions.[38] The Negrians *want* Empire to take a juridical form, they *want* to have a personal sovereignty sitting across from them, an institutional subject with which to enter into contract or take over power. The "global civil society" that they call for merely betrays their *desire* for a global State. Sure, they proffer some proof, or what they believe to be proof, for the existence of a coming universal order: the imperial interventions in Kosovo, in Somalia, or in the Gulf, and their spectacular legitimization in "universal values." But even if Empire could endow itself with a fake institutional facade, its actual reality would still remain concentrated in worldwide police and publicity, or, respectively, Biopower and Spectacle. The fact that the imperial wars present themselves as "international police operations" implemented by "intervention forces," the fact that war itself is put outside the law by a form of domination that wants to pass off its own military offensives as little more than domestic administration, that is, as a police and not a political matter—to ensure "tranquility, security, and order"—all this Schmitt had already anticipated sixty years ago, and in no way does it contribute to the gradual development of a "right of the police," as Negri would like to believe. The momentary spectacular consensus against this or that "rogue State," this or that "dictator" or "terrorist" only validates the temporary and reversible legitimacy of any imperial intervention that appeals to this consensus. The restaging of degraded Nuremberg Trials for any and every reason, the unilateral decision made by the national judiciaries to judge crimes that have taken place in countries where the judiciaries are not even recognized as such does not confirm the advancement of a nascent global right, but the complete subordination of the juridical order to a state of emergency wrought by the police. In conditions like this, it is not a question of agitating in support of a salutary universal State, but instead of demolishing Spectacle and Biopower.

64 As we are beginning to recognize, imperial domination can be described as *neotaoist*, since it is only in this tradition that it has been completely thought through. Twenty-three centuries ago a Taoist theoretician asserted the following: "Means the sage employs to lead to political order are three. The first is said to be profit; the second, authority; and the third, fame. Profit is the means whereby the people's hearts are won; authority is the means whereby to enforce orders; denomination is the common way linking superior and inferior. […] this can be said to abolish government by means of government, abolish words by means of words."[39] Mincing no words, he concluded: "In the perfect government, inferiors have no virtue" (Han Fei Tzu).[40] Indeed government is quite likely perfected.

GLOSS: There are those who have wanted to describe the imperial period as a time of slaves without masters. Even if this is not entirely false, it would be better to describe it as a time *of Mastery without masters*, of the nonexistent sovereign, like Calvino's nonexistent knight, who was nothing but an empty suit of armor. The place of the Prince remains, invisibly occupied by *the principle*. There is in this both an absolute rupture with and a fulfillment of the old personal sovereignty: the Master's greatest dismay has always been to have nothing but slaves for subjects. The reigning Principle carries off the paradox to which substantive sovereignty had had to yield: *to have one's slaves be free men*. This empty sovereignty is not, properly speaking, an historical novelty, even if it is in the West. The task here is to break with the metaphysics of subjectivity. The Chinese, who established themselves outside of the metaphysics of subjectivity between the sixth and third century BCE, at that time formed a theory of impersonal sovereignty that is not unhelpful for understanding the current motives of imperial domination. Closely associated with this theory is the name of Han Fei Tzu, the key figure in the school known as "legalism," although this is misleading as his contributions concern more the norm than the Law. His teachings, today collected under the title "The Tao of the Sovereign," are what motivated the founding of the first truly unified Chinese Empire, and what brought an end to the period of the "Warring States." Once the Empire was established, the Emperor, the Ch'in sovereign, had the works of Han Fei burned in 213 BCE. Only in the twentieth century was the text unearthed, a text that had prescribed the practices of the Chinese Empire at the very moment it was collapsing.

Han Fei's Prince, he who holds the Position, is Prince solely because of his impersonality, because of his absence of qualities, because of his invisibility, his inactivity; he is only Prince to the extent that he is absorbed in the Tao, into the Way, into the flow of things. He is not a Prince in the sense of a person, he is a Principle, a pure void, that occupies the Position and dwells in non-acting. For a "legalist" Empire, the State should be completely immanent to civil society: "keeping the state safe is like having food when hungry and clothes when cold, not by will but by nature,"[41] explains Han Fei. The function of the sovereign is here to articulate the apparatuses that will make him unnecessary, that will allow cybernetic self-regulation. If, in some respects, the teachings of Han Fei evoke certain formulations from liberal thought, it refuses their false naiveté: the teachings present themselves as a theory of absolute domination. Han Fei exhorts the Prince to abide by the Way of Lao Tzu: "Heaven and Earth are ruthless; they treat the myriad creatures as straw dogs. The sage is ruthless; he treats the people as straw dogs."[42] Even his most faithful ministers must know how insignificant they are in the eyes of the Imperial Machine—the same ministers, who only yesterday believed themselves masters—must dread that some crusade to "moralize public life" might swoop down on them, some craving for transparency. The art of imperial domination entails being absorbed in the Principle, fading away into nothingness, seeing everything by becoming invisible, holding everything by becoming ungraspable. The withdrawal of the Prince is here nothing but the withdrawal of the Principle: establish the norms by which beings will be judged and evaluated, make sure that things are named in the "appropriate" way, regulate rewards and punishments, govern identities and attach men to them. Keep to this and remain opaque: such is the art of empty and dematerialized domination, of the *imperial* domination of withdrawal.

"Tao exists in invisibility; its function, in unintelligibility. Be empty and reposed and have nothing to do. Then from the dark see defects in the light. See but never be seen. Hear but never be heard. Know but never be known. If you hear any word uttered, do not change it nor move it but compare it with the deed and see if word and deed coincide with each other. Place every official with a censor. Do not let them speak to each other. Then everything will be exerted to the utmost. Cover tracks and conceal sources. Then the ministers cannot trace origins. Leave your wisdom and cease your ability. Then your subordinates cannot guess at your limitations.

"Keep your decision and identify it with the words and deeds of your subordinates. Cautiously take the handles and hold them fast. Uproot others' want of them, smash others' thought of them, and do not let anybody covet them. [...]

"The Tao of the lord of men regards tranquillity and humility as treasures. Without handling anything himself, he can tell skilfulness from unskilfulness [sic]; without his own concerns of mind, he can tell good from bad luck. Therefore, without uttering any word himself, he finds a good reply given; without exerting his own effort, he finds his task accomplished."[43]

—Han Fei Tzu, "The Tao of the Sovereign"

"The sceptre should never be shown. For its inner nature is non-assertion. The state affairs may be scattered in the four directions but the key to their administration is in the centre. The sage holding this key in hand, people from the four directions come to render him meritorious services. He remains empty and waits for their services, and they will exert their abilities by themselves. With the conditions of the four seas clearly in mind, he can see the Yang by means of the Yin. [...] He can go onward with the two handles without making any change. To apply them without cessation is said to be acting on the right way of government.

"Indeed, everything has its function; every material has its utility. When everybody works according to his special qualification, both superior and inferior will not have to do anything. Let roosters herald the dawn and let cats watch for rats. When everything exercises its special qualification, the ruler will not have to do anything. [...]

"The way to assume oneness starts from the study of terminology. When names are rectified, things will be settled. [...] Therefore, he promotes them through an examination of names. [...]

"If his own wisdom and talent are not discarded, it will be hard for him to keep a constant principle of government. [...]

"The ruler of men should often stretch the tree but never allow its branches to flourish."[44]

—Han Fei Tzu, "Wielding the Sceptre"

65 All imperial strategies—whether the spectacular polarization of bodies toward various suitable absences or the constant terror ONE doggedly maintains—seek to ensure that Empire never appears as such, namely, as *party*. This peculiar kind of peace, this *armed* peace characteristic of imperial order, is felt to be all the more oppressive because it is itself the result of a total, mute, and continuous war. The stakes of the offensive are not to win a certain confrontation, but rather to make sure that the confrontation *does not take place*, to eliminate the event at the source, to prevent any surge of intensity in the play of forms-of-life through which the political might occur. It is a huge victory for Empire if nothing happens. Faced with "whatever enemy," faced with the Imaginary Party, its strategy is to "replace the events that one would like to be decisive but which remain unpredictable (i.e. battle) with a series of minor but statistically consistent actions that we call, by contrast, non-battle" (Guy Brossollet, *Essai sur la non-bataille*, 1975).[45]

66 Empire does not confront us like a subject, facing us, but like an *environment* that is hostile to us.

An Ethic of Civil War

New form of community, asserting itself in a warlike manner. Otherwise the spirit grows soft. No "gardens" and no sheer "evasion in the face of the masses." War (but without gunpowder!) between different thoughts! and their armies![46]

— Nietzsche, "Posthumous Fragments"

67 All those who cannot or will not conjure away the forms-of-life that move them must come to grips with the following fact: they are, we are, the *pariahs* of Empire. Anchored somewhere within us, there is a lightless spot, a mark of Cain filling citizens with terror if not outright hatred. This is the Manichaeism of Empire: on one side there is the glorious new humanity, carefully reformatted, thrown open to all the rays of power, ideally lacking in experience, and oblivious to themselves until they become cancerous. These are citizens, the citizens of Empire. And then there's *us*. Us—it is neither a subject, nor something formed, nor a multitude. Us—it is a heap of worlds, of sub-spectacular and interstitial worlds, whose existence is unmentionable, woven together with the kind of solidarity and dissent that power cannot penetrate; and there are the strays, the poor, the prisoners, the thieves, the criminals, the crazy, the perverts, the corrupted, the overly alive, the overflowing, the rebellious corporalities. In short, all those who, following their own line of flight, do not fit into Empire's stale, air-conditioned paradise. *Us*—this is the fragmented plane of consistency of the Imaginary Party.

68 Insofar as we stay in contact with our own potentiality, even if only in thinking through our experience, we represent a danger within the metropolises of Empire. We are *whatever enemy* against which all the imperial apparatuses and norms are positioned. Conversely, the resentful ones, the intellectual, the immunodeficient, the humanist, the transplant patient, the neurotic are Empire's model citizens. From these citizens, THEY are certain there is nothing to fear. Given their circumstances, these citizens are lashed to a set of artificial conditions of existence, such that only Empire can guarantee their survival; any dramatic shift in their conditions of existence and they die. They are born collaborators. It is not only power that passes through their bodies, but also the police. This kind of mutilated life arises not only as a consequence of Empire's progress, but as its *precondition*. The equation *citizen = cop* runs deep within the crack that exists at the core of such bodies.

69 Everything allowed by Empire is for us similarly limited: spaces, words, loves, heads, and hearts. So many nooses around the neck. Wherever we go quarantine lines of petrification spring up almost spontaneously all around us; we feel it in how they look and act. The slightest thing is all it takes to be identified as a suspect by Empire's anemic citizens, to be identified as a *risky dividual*. There is a never ending haggling over whether we will renounce the intimate relationship that we have with ourselves, something for which THEY have given us so much flak. And indeed, we will not hold out forever like this, in this tormented role of the domestic deserter, of the stateless alien, of such a carefully concealed hostis.

70 To the citizens of Empire, we have nothing to say. That would mean we shared something in common. As far as they are concerned, the choice is clear: either desert, join us and throw yourself into becoming, or stay where you are and be dealt with in accordance with the well-known principles of hostility: reduction and abasement.

71 For us, the *hostis* is this very hostility that, within Empire, orders both the non-relation to self and the generalized non-relation between bodies. Anything that tries to arouse in us this hostis must be annihilated. What I mean is that the sphere of hostility itself must be reduced.

72 The only way to reduce the sphere of hostility is by spreading the ethico-political domain of friendship and enmity. This is why Empire has never been able to reduce this sphere of hostility, despite all its clamoring in the name of peace. The becoming-real of the Imaginary Party is simply the formation—the *contagious* formation—of a plane of consistency where friendships and enmities can freely deploy themselves and make themselves legible to each other.

73 An agent of the imaginary Party is someone who, wherever he is, from his own *position*, triggers or pursues the process of ethical polarization, the differential assumption of forms-of-life. This process is nothing other than *tiqqun*.

74 Tiqqun is the becoming-real, the becoming-*practice* of the world. Tiqqun is the process through which everything is revealed to be practice, that is, to take place within its own limits, within its own immanent signification. Tiqqun means that each act, conduct, and statement endowed with sense—act, conduct and statement as *event*—spontaneously manifests its own metaphysics, its own community, its own *party*. Civil war simply means the world is practice, and life is, in its smallest details, heroic.

75 The defeat of the revolutionary movement was not, as Stalinists always complain, due to its lack of unity. It was defeated because the civil war within its ranks was not worked out with enough force. The crippling effects of the systematic confusion between hostis and enemy are self-evident, whether it be the tragedy of the Soviet Union or the groupuscular comedy.

Let's be clear. Empire is not the enemy with which we have to contend, and other tendencies within the Imaginary Party are not, for us, so many hostis to be eliminated. The opposite is, in fact, the case.

76 Every form-of-life tends to constitute a community, and as a community tends to constitute a world. Each world, when it thinks itself—when it grasps itself strategically in its play with other worlds—discovers that it is structured by a particular metaphysics which is, more than a system, *a language, its* language. When a world thinks itself, it becomes infectious. It knows the ethic it carries within, and it has mastered, within its domain, the art of distances.

77 For each body, the most intense serenity is found by pushing its present form-of-life to the limit, all the way to the point where the line disappears, the line along which its power grows. Each body wants to exhaust its form-of-life and leave it for dead. Then, it passes on to another. This is how a body gets thicker, nourished with experience. But it also becomes more supple: it has learned how to get rid of one figure of the self.

78 There where bare life was, the form-of-life should come to be. Sickness and weakness do not really happen to bare life in its generic sense. They are affections that touch, in a singular way, specific forms-of-life, and are scripted by the contradictory imperatives of imperial pacification. If we manage to bring everything THEY exile to the confused language of bare life back home to the terrain of forms-of-life, we can invert biopolitics into a *politics of radical singularity*. We have to reinvent the field of health, and invent a *political* medicine based on forms-of-life.

79 Under the current conditions imposed by Empire, an ethical grouping has to turn itself into a *war machine*. The object of the war machine is not war. To the contrary, it can "make war only on the condition that they simultaneously create something else, if only new nonorganic social relations" (Deleuze, *A Thousand Plateaus*).[47] Unlike an army or revolutionary *organizations*, the war machine has a *supplemental* relation to war. It is capable of offensive exploits and can enter into battle; it can have unlimited recourse to violence. But it does not *need* this to lead a full, complete existence.

80 This is where the question of taking back both violence and all the intense expressions of life stolen from us by biopolitical democracies has to be posed. We should start by getting rid of the tired idea that death always comes at the end, as the final moment of life. Death is *everyday*, it is the continuous diminution of our presence that occurs when we no longer have the strength to abandon ourselves to our inclinations. Each wrinkle and each illness is some taste we have betrayed, some infidelity to a form-of-life animating us. This is our real death, and its chief cause is our lack of strength, the *isolation* that prevents us from trading blows with power, which forbids us from letting go of ourselves without the assurance we will have to pay for it. Our bodies feel the need to gather together into war machines, for this alone makes it possible *to live and to struggle*.

81 It should now be clear that, in the biopolitical sense, there is no such thing as a "natural" death. All deaths are *violent*. Both existentially and historically speaking. Under the biopolitical democracies of Empire, everything has been socialized, and each death is inserted into a complex network of causalities that make it a *social* death, a murder. Today, there is only murder, whether it is condemned, pardoned, or, most often, denied. At this point, there is no longer any question about the *fact* of murder, only about *how* it happens.

82 The fact is nothing, the *how* is all. The proof is that facts must be *qualified* beforehand, in order to be facts. Spectacle's genius is to have acquired a monopoly over qualifications, over the *act of naming*. With this in hand, it can then smuggle in its metaphysics and pass off the products of its fraudulent interpretations as facts. Some act of social war gets called a "terrorist act," while a major intervention by NATO, initiated through the most arbitrary process, is deemed a "peacekeeping operation." Mass poisonings are described as epidemics, while the "High-Security Wing" is the technical term used in our democracies' prisons for the legal practice of torture. *Tiqqun* is, to the contrary, the action that restores to each fact its *how*, of holding this how to be the *only real* there is. A death by duel, a fine assassination, or a last brilliant phrase uttered with pathos would be enough to clean up the blood and humanize what ONE says is the height of inhumanity—murder. In murder more than anything, the fact is absorbed by the *how*. Between enemies, for example, no firearms are allowed.

83 This world is pulled between two tendencies: Lebanonization and Swissification. These tendencies can coexist and alternate zone by zone. Indeed, these two seemingly opposed yet reversible tendencies represent two ways of warding off civil war. After all, before 1974, wasn't Lebanon nicknamed the "Switzerland of the Middle East"?

84 In the becoming-real of the Imaginary Party, we will no doubt cross paths with those ghastly parasites, the professional revolutionaries. Even though the only beautiful moments of the last century were disparagingly called "civil wars," they will no doubt still denounce in us "the conspiracy of the ruling class to break down the revolution by a civil war" (Marx, *The Civil War in France*).[48] We do not believe in the revolution, we believe a bit more in "molecular revolutions," and wholeheartedly believe in the differentiated ways of taking up civil war. The professional revolutionaries—whose repeated disasters have hardly discouraged them—will first of all smear us as dilettantes and as traitors to the Cause. They will want us to think that Empire is the enemy. We will answer Their Stupidity by pointing out that Empire is not the enemy, it is the *hostis*. It is not a matter of defeating Empire, it has to be annihilated; and if need be we can do without their Party, following the advice of Clausewitz on the subject of popular war: "A general uprising, as we see it, should be nebulous and elusive; its resistance should never materialize as a concrete body, otherwise the enemy can direct sufficient force as its core, crush it, and take many prisoners. When that happens, the people will lose heart and, believing that the issue has been decided and further efforts would be useless, drop their weapons. On the other hand, there must be some concentration at certain points: the fog must thicken and form a dark and menacing cloud out of which a bolt of lightning may strike at any time. These points for concentration will, as we have said, lie mainly on the flanks of the enemy's theater of operations. [...] They are not supposed to pulverize the core but to nibble at the shell and around the edges" (*On War*).[49]

85 The preceding phrases will usher in a new era that will be shadowed, in ever more tangible ways, by the threat of a sudden unleashing of reality. At some point, the "Invisible Committee" was the name given to the ethic of civil war expressed in these pages. It refers to a specific faction of the Imaginary Party, its revolutionary-experimental wing. We hope that with these lines we can avoid some of the cruder inanities that might be formulated about the nature of our activities and about the era just now dawning. Can't we already hear this predictable chatter in the opinion held of the Muromachi period at the end of the Tokugawa shogunate, described so well by one of our enemies: "This era of civil wars, precisely because of its turmoil and the swelling of its out-sized ambitions, turned out to be the freest ever known in Japan. All sorts of shady figures let themselves get caught up in it. And this is why so many have stressed the fact that it was simply the most violent of eras"?

How Is It to Be Done?

Don't know what I want,
but I know how to get it.

— Sex Pistols, *Anarchy in the UK*

1

TWENTY YEARS. Twenty years *of counter-revolution.*
Of *preventive* counter-revolution.
In Italy.
And elsewhere.
Twenty years of a sleep studded with fences, haunted by
security guards. A sleep of *bodies,*
imposed by curfew.
Twenty years. The past does not pass. Because the
war continues. Ramifies. Extends.
In a global reticulation of local apparatuses. In a
newfound calibration of subjectivities.
Within a new superficial peace.
An *armed* peace
crafted to cover the uncoiling of an imperceptible
civil war.

Twenty years ago, there was
punk, the Movement of '77, the "area" of Autonomy,
the metropolitan Indians and diffuse guerrilla warfare.
All at once there sprung up,
as if issuing from some underground region of
civilization,
an entire counter-world of subjectivities

that no longer wanted to consume, that no longer
wanted to produce,
that no longer even wanted to be subjectivities.
The revolution was molecular, and so was the
counter-revolution.
On the offensive, THEY set up,
then left in place,
an entire complex machine to neutralize all that carries
intense charge. A machine for defusing all that *might*
explode.
All the dividuals that pose a risk,
the intractable bodies,
the autonomous human aggregations.
Then came twenty years of foolishness, vulgarity,
isolation, and desolation.
How is it to be done?

Get back up. Pick *your head* up. By choice or by
necessity. No matter, really, from now on.
Look each other in the eyes and say we are starting
over. Let everyone know it, as quickly as possible.
We are starting over.
We are done with passive resistance, inner exile,
conflict through subtraction, survival. We are starting
over. In twenty years, we have had time to see. We
have understood. Demokracy for all, the "anti-terrorist"
struggle, the State massacres, the capitalist restructuring
and its Great Work of social purging,
by selection,
by precariousness,

by normalization,
by "modernization."
We have seen, we have understood. The means and
the ends. The future held in store for us. The one
we have been denied. The state of exception. The law
that puts the police, civil servants, public officials
above the law. The growing judicialization,
psychiatrization, the medicalization of all that is
out of bounds. Of all that *flees*.
We have seen. We have understood. The means and
the ends.

When power establishes its own legitimacy in real time,
when its violence becomes preventive
and its right is a "right to intervene,"
then it is now useless to be right. To be right *against it*.
One must be stronger, or more clever. This is also
why
we are starting over.

To start over is never to begin *something* again. Nor
to pick up things where they had been left off.
What one begins again is always *something else*. Is
always unprecedented. Because it is not the past
that drives us, but precisely what in it
has not
happened.
And because it is also *ourselves*, then, that we start
over with.
To begin again means: to exit the suspension. To

reestablish contact between our becomings.
To start out from,
once again,
wherever we are,
now.

For instance, there are some rackets
that THEY will not pull on us anymore.
The "society" racket. Transform it. Destroy it.
Make it better.
The social pact racket. That some would break and
others pretend to "restore" it.
These rackets, THEY will not pull them on us anymore.
You have to be a militant element of the planetary
petty bourgeoisie,
a *citizen* really
Not to see that it, society, no longer
exists.
That it has imploded. That it is nothing more than
an argument for the terror of those who claim to
re/present it.
This society that has turned up missing.
All that is social has become foreign to us.
We consider ourselves absolutely unbound to any
obligation, to any prerogative, to any belonging that is
social.
"Society,"
is the name the Irreparable has often received
from those who also wanted to turn it into
the Unassumable.

He who refuses this lure will have to take
a step to the side.
To perform
a slight shift away
from the logic common
to Empire and to its contestation,
that of *mobilization*,
A step to the side of their common temporality,
that of *urgency*.

Starting over means: inhabiting this gap. To take on
the capitalist schizophrenia as a kind of growing
capacity for *desubjectivization*.
To desert *while keeping arms*.
To flee, imperceptibly.
Starting over means: to rally social secession, opacity,
to enter
into demobilization,
Ripping off, from this or that imperial network of
production-consumption, the means to live and
fight in order, at the chosen moment,
to scuttle it.

We speak of a new war,
a new war *of partisans*. With neither front nor
uniform, with neither army nor decisive battle.
A war whose focii concentrate themselves away
from the commercial flows, while still remaining
plugged in to them.
We speak of a completely latent war. That *has time*.

Of a war of *position*.
That is waged here where we are.
In the name of no one.
In the name of our own existence,
which has no name.

Perform this slight shift.
No longer fear our time.
"Not to fear one's time is a question of space."
In a squat. In an orgy. In a riot. In a train or an
occupied village. In search of, amid unknowns, a
free party that is unfindable. I experience this slight
shift. The experience
of my desubjectivization. I *become*
a whatever singularity. Some *play* opens up between
my presence and the whole apparatus of qualities
that are ordinarily attached to me.
In the eyes of a being who, being present, wants to
assess me *for what I am*, I savor the disappointment,
his disappointment in seeing me become so *common*,
so perfectly *accessible*. In the gestures of another, it
is an unexpected complicity.
All that isolates me as a *subject*, as a body endowed
with a public configuration of attributes, I feel it
founder. Bodies brush up against each other at their
edges. At their edges, are indistinct. Neighborhood
after neighborhood, the whatever lays waste to
equivalence. And I reach a new nakedness,
a nakedness that is *not my own*, as if clothed in love.
Does one ever escape alone from the prison of the Self?

In a squat. In an orgy. In a riot. In a train or an occupied village. We meet again.
We meet again
as whatever singularities. That is to say
not on the basis of a common belonging,
but of a *common presence.*
Thus is
our *need for communism.* The need for nocturnal spaces, where we can
meet up
beyond
our predicates.
Beyond the *tyranny* of recognition. Which imposes re/cognition as the *final* distance between bodies.
As an unavoidable separation.
Everything THEY—fiancé, family, environment, business, the State, public opinion—recognize in me, THEY use to seize hold of me.
By constantly reminding me of what I am, of my *qualities,* THEY would like to abstract me from each situation. In every circumstance, THEY would like to extort from me a fidelity to myself which is a fidelity *to my predicates.*
THEY expect that I should act as a man, as an employee, as an unemployed person, as a mother, as an activist, or as a philosopher.
THEY want to contain within the bounds of an identity the unpredictable flow of my becomings.
THEY want to convert me to the religion of a coherence that THEY chose for me.

The more I am *recognized*, the more my gestures are hindered, hindered *from within*. And here I am caught in the ultra-tight meshwork of the new power. In the impalpable snares of the new police: THE IMPERIAL POLICE OF QUALITIES.

There is a whole network of apparatuses that I slip into in order to "integrate" myself, and which *incorporate* in me these qualities.

A whole little system of filing, identification, and mutual policing.

A whole diffuse prescription of absence.

A whole machinery of comport/mental control, aiming toward panopticism, toward transparent privatization, toward atomization.

And in which I struggle.

I need to become anonymous. In order to be present. *The more I am anonymous, the more I am present.*

I need zones of indistinction
in order to reach the Common.

To no longer *recognize* myself in my name. To no longer hear in my name anything but the voice that calls it.

To give consistency to the *how* of beings, not what they are, but *how* they are what they are. Their form-of-life.

I need zones of opacity where attributes,
even criminal, even brilliant,
no longer separate bodies.

Become whatever. Becoming a whatever *singularity* is not given.

Always possible, but never given.
There is a *politics* of whatever singularity.
Which consists in tearing back from Empire
the conditions and the means,
even interstitial,
to experience yourself as such.
This is a politics, because it presupposes a capacity
for confrontation,
and because a new human aggregation
corresponds to it.
Politics of whatever singularity: freeing up these
spaces where an action is no longer assignable to
any given body.
Where bodies rediscover their aptitude for *gesture*,
something that the canny distribution of metropolitan
apparatuses—computers, automobiles, schools,
cameras, mobile phones, sports arenas, hospitals,
televisions, cinemas, etc.—had stolen from them.
By recognizing them.
By immobilizing them.
By letting them spin against nothing.
By making the head exist separately from the body.
Politics of whatever singularity.
A becoming-whatever is more revolutionary than
any kind of being-whatever.
Liberating spaces liberates us a hundred times more
than any kind of "liberated space."
More than putting a power into action, I enjoy the
circulation of my potentiality.
The politics of whatever singularity lies in the

offensive. In the circumstances, the moments, and
the places where we tear away
the circumstances, the moments, and the places
for such an anonymity,
for a momentary halt in a state of simplicity,
the chance to extract from all our forms *the pure
adequation to presence*,
the chance to be, at last,
here.

2

How is it to be done? Not *What is to be done?*
How to? A question of means.
Not a question of goals, or *objectives*,
of what there is *to do*, strategically, in the absolute.
A question of what one *can* do, tactically, in a situation,
and of the *acquisition* of this power.
How is it to be done? How to desert? How does it work?
How to conjugate my wounds with communism?
How to stay at war without losing our tenderness?
The question is technical. Not a problem. Problems
are profitable.
The experts live off them.
A question.
Technical. Which requires in turn the question of
transmission techniques for those techniques.
How is it to be done? The result always belies the
goal. Because to set a goal
is still a means,
another means.

What Is to Be Done? Babeuf, Chernyshevsky, Lenin.
Classical virility demands an analgesic, a mirage,
something. A *means* to ignore oneself a bit more.

As a presence.

As a form-of-life. As a being *in a situation*, endowed with inclinations.

Determined inclinations.

What is to be done? Voluntarism as the ultimate nihilism. As the nihilism appropriate *to classical virility*.

What is to be done? The answer is simple: submit once again to the logic of mobilization, to the temporality of urgency. Under pretext of rebellion. Set down ends, *words*. Tend toward their accomplishment. Toward the accomplishment *of words*. In the meantime, put off existing. Bracket yourself. Dwell in the exception of self. Separated from time. That passes. That does not pass. That stops. Until… Until the next. End.

What is to be done? In other words: useless to live. Everything you have not lived, History will give back to you.

What is to be done? It is the forgetting of the self projected onto the world.

As a forgetting of the world.

How is it to be done? The question is *how*. Not *what* a being, a gesture, a thing *is*, but *how* it is what it is. How its predicates relate to it.

And it to them.

Let it be. Leave the gap between the subject and its predicates. The *abyss* of presence.

A man is not "a man." "White horse" is not "horse."
A question of *how*. *Attention* to the *how*. Attention
to the way a woman is, and is not,
a woman—it takes apparatuses to make "a woman"
of a sexually female being, or "a Black" of a man
with black skin.
Attention to *ethical difference*. To the ethical *element*.
To the irreducibilities that traverse it. What
happens between bodies during an occupation is
more interesting than the occupation itself.
How is it to be done? means that military confrontation
with Empire must be subordinated to the
intensification of relations within our party. That
the political is only a certain degree of intensity
amidst the ethical element. That revolutionary war
should no longer be confused with its
representation: the raw moment of combat.

Question of *how*. Become attentive to the taking-
place of things, of beings. To their event. To the
obstinate and silent salience of their
own temporality
beneath the planetary flattening of all temporalities
by the time of urgency.
The "*What is to be done?*" as programmatic ignorance
of all that. As inaugural formula
for frantically falling out of love.

The "*What is to be done?*" returns. For some years now.
Since the middle of the nineties, not just since Seattle.

A revival of *critique* pretends to confront Empire
with slogans, recipes from the sixties. Except that
this time, they're faking it.
Innocence, indignation, good conscience, and the need
for society are simulated. The old gamut of social-
democratic affects are back in circulation. *Christian* affects.
And once again, there are demonstrations. Desire-
killing demonstrations. Where nothing happens.
That only demonstrate
a collective absence.
Forever.

For those nostalgic for Woodstock, weed, May '68
and militancy, there are counter-summits. THEY
have rebuilt the facades, *minus the possible*.
This is what the "*What Is to Be Done?*" demands
today: go to the ends of the earth to contest the
global commodity
only to come back, after a long bath of unanimity
and mediatized separation,
and submit to the local commodity.
Once back, there's a photo in the paper... Everyone
alone together!... Once upon a time...
These young people!...
Too bad for the few living bodies that strayed there,
searching in vain for a space for their desire.
They come back a little more bored. A little more
empty. Worn out.
From counter-summit to counter-summit,
they will figure it out. Or not.

Empire can't be faulted for its management. You can't *critique* Empire.

You *oppose* its forces.

Wherever you are.

Giving your opinion on some alternative, going wherever ONE calls us——this no longer makes sense. There is no global project that would be an alternative to the global project of Empire. Because there is no global project of Empire.

There is an *imperial management.*

There is no good management.

Those who call for another society would do better by beginning to see that there is no longer such a thing.

And maybe then they'll stop being managers-in-training.

Citizens. *Indignant* citizens.

You can't take the global order for an enemy. Not directly.

For the global order has no place. To the contrary.

It is the order of non-places.

It is perfect not because it is global, but because it is *globally local.* The global order is the warding off of every event, it is the complete, authoritarian occupation of the local.

You can only oppose the global order *locally.* By extending shadowy zones over the maps of Empire. And by progressively putting them into contact. Underground.

The coming politics. Politics of local insurrection against global management. The triumph of presence over absence to self. Over the imperial estrangement of the citizen.

Presence triumphing through theft, fraud, crime, friendship, enmity, conspiracy.

Through the elaboration of modes of life that are also modes of struggle.

Politics of taking-place.

Empire *does not take place*. It administers absence through a hovering threat of police intervention. Whoever tries to measure up against the imperial adversary will be preventively annihilated.

From now on, to be perceived is to be defeated.

Learn to become indiscernible. Blend in. Revive the taste
for anonymity,
for promiscuity.
Renounce distinction
in order to evade repression:
arrange for the most favorable conditions of confrontation.
Become crafty. Become pitiless. To do so,
become whatever.

How is it to be done? is a question for the lost children. Those who haven't been told. Whose gestures are awkward. To whom nothing has been *given*. Whose creatureness, whose wandering never stops revealing itself.

The coming revolt is the revolt of lost children.

The transmission line of history has snapped.

Orphans of the revolutionary tradition itself. The worker's movement above all. The worker's movement that was transformed into an instrument of greater integration into the Process. Into the new, cybernetic, Process of social valorization.

In 1978, in the name of this Process, the Italian Communist Party, the "party with clean hands," started hunting down Autonomia.

In the name of its classist conception of the proletariat, its mysticism of society, its respect for work, the useful and the decent.

In the name of defending "democratic gains" and the rule of law.

The worker's movement that survived up to *operaismo*. Sole existing critique of capitalism *from the point of view of Total Mobilization*.

Formidable and paradoxical doctrine,

that ended up saving objectivist Marxism by only speaking of "subjectivity."

That introduced new refinements in the denegation of the *how*.

The reabsorption of the gesture in its product.

The allergy of the *future anterior*.

That everything *will have been*.

Critique has become vain. Critique has become vain because it amounts to an absence. With the

dominant order, everyone knows what to expect.
We no longer need *critical* theory. We no longer
need teachers. From now on, critique works for
domination. *Even the critique of domination.*
It reproduces absence. It speak to us from where we
are not. It drives us somewhere else. It consumes
us. It is cowardly.
And stays safe
when it sends us to slaughter.
Secretly in love with its object, it never stops lying
to us.
Hence such brief affairs between proletarians and
committed intellectuals.
Marriages of convenience, *reasonable*, where neither
has the same idea of pleasure or freedom.

Rather than new critiques, new cartographies
are what we need.
Cartographies not for Empire, but for lines of flight
out of it.
How is it to be done? We need maps. Not maps of
what is off the map.
We need navigation maps. *Maritime* maps. Tools
for *orientation*. That don't try to say or represent
what is within different archipelagoes of desertion,
but show us how to meet up with them.
Portolan charts.

3

It is Tuesday, March 17, 1996, just before dawn.
The ROS (Special Operations Group) co-ordinates
the arrest up and down the peninsula
of 70 Italian anarchists.
Their aim is to put an end to 15 years of fruitless
investigations of insurrectional anarchists.
The technique is well-known: fabricate a "turn-
coat," have him disclose the existence of a vast,
hierarchical organization of subversives.
Then, on the basis of this made-up construction,
accuse everyone you want to neutralize of being
part of it.
Once again, drain the sea to catch some fish.
Even when it's only a small pond.
And small fry.

An ROS "internal memorandum" was leaked
regarding this affair.
It revealed the strategy.
Founded on the principles of General Dalla Chiesa,
the ROS is a classic example of the imperial agency
of counter-insurrection.
It works on the population.

Wherever some intensity occurs, wherever
something happens, it is the "French Doctor" of
the situation.[1] The one who unfurls,
claiming it is a preventive measure,
the *cordon sanitaires* that will isolate
the contagion.
When it's scared, it says so. In this document, it
spells it out. What it's scared of is the "swamp of
political anonymity."
Empire is afraid.
Empire is afraid that we'll become whatever. A
delimited space,
a fighting force. These it has no fear of. It is afraid
of an expansive constellation of squats, of self-
managed farms, collective houses, *fine a se stesso*
gatherings, radios, skills, and ideas. The whole
bound together by an intense circulation of bodies
and affects between
bodies. Which is something else entirely.

Conspiracy of bodies. Not critical minds, but *critical
corporealities.* That's what Empire is scared of.
That's what's slowly coming about,
with the increasing flow
of social defection.
There is an opacity inherent to the *contact* between
bodies. And that is incompatible with the imperial
reign of a light that no longer illuminates things
except to break them down.
Zones of Offensive Opacity do not have

to be created.
They are already there, in any kind of relation that brings about a veritable
putting into play of bodies.
What's needed is to *embrace* the fact that we take part in this opacity. And to give ourselves the means to spread it,
defend it.
Everywhere you manage to sidestep the imperial apparatuses, to ruin all the daily work of Biopower and the Spectacle in order to extricate a fraction of citizens from the population. To isolate new *untorelli*.[2] In this indistinction that's won back, an autonomous ethical tissue,
a secessionist
plane of consistency
spontaneously forms.
Bodies gather. Get their breath back. Conspire.
That such zones are doomed to be flattened militarily means little. What matters is that each time we arrange a fairly secure escape route. In order to gather together again elsewhere.
Later.
Behind the question *What is to be done?* was the *myth* of the general strike.
Answering the question *How is it to be done?* is the *practice* of the HUMAN STRIKE.
The general strike says that operations are limited in space and time,
a piecemeal alienation, thanks to a recognizable,

and therefore defeatable, enemy.

The human strike corresponds to an era when the borders between work and life have become blurred.

When consuming and surviving,
producing "subversive texts" and protecting against the most toxic effects of industrial civilization,
playing sports, making love, being a parent or being on Prozac.
Everything is work.
For Empire manages, digests, absorbs and reintegrates all that lives.
Even "what I am," the subjectivation I don't refute *hic et nunc,*
all is productive.
Empire has put everything to work.
Ideally, my professional profile will coincide with my own face.
Even if it's not smiling.
The grimaces of the rebel sell quite well, after all.

Empire is when the means of production have become the means of control and the means of control the means of production.
Empire signifies that henceforth the political moment *dominates*
the economic moment.
And the general strike is powerless against it.
What must be opposed to Empire is
the human strike.

Which never attacks the relations of production
without attacking at the same time the affective
relations that sustain it.
Which undermines the unavowable libidinal
economy,
restores the ethical element—the *how*—repressed in
every contact between neutralized bodies.
The human strike is the strike that, whenever THEY
expect
this or that predictable reaction,
some contrite or indignant tone,
PREFERS NOT TO.
Slips away from the apparatus. Saturates it, or
blows it away.
Gets ahold of itself, preferring
something else.
Something else that is not limited to the possibilities
authorized by the apparatus.
At the counter of some government office, at the
checkout counter of some grocery store, in a polite
conversation, when the cops intervene,
following the relations of force,
the human strike gives consistency to the space
between bodies,
pulverizes the *double bind* that holds them,
drives them to presence.
A new Luddism must be invented, a Luddism
against the human gears
that turn the wheels of Capital.

In Italy, radical feminism was an embryonic form of the human strike.

"No more mothers, wives or daughters, let's destroy the family!" was an invitation to make the gesture of breaking the predictable chains of events,
of liberating compressed possibilities.
It targeted shitty affective exchanges, everyday prostitution.
It was a call to get beyond the couple, the elementary unit of the management of alienation.
Call for complicity, then.
Practice that is untenable without circulation, without contagion.
The women's strike implicitly called for a strike by men and children, called to empty the factories, schools, offices and prisons,
to reinvent for each situation another way of being—another *how*.
In the 1970s, Italy was an enormous human strike zone.
Self-reductions, holdups, squatted neighborhoods, armed demonstrations, pirate radio, untold cases of "Stockholm syndrome,"
even the famous letters sent by Moro when he was a hostage, toward the end,
practiced the human strike.
Back then, the Stalinists were talking about "diffuse irrationality," which says it all.

There are also writers

for whom it is always
the human strike.
In Kafka, in Walser;
or in Michaux,
for example.

Acquire *collectively* the ability to shake out the
familiar.
The art of feeling at home
with the most uncanny of all guests.

In the present war,
where Capital's emergency reformism has to don
the revolutionary's clothes to make itself heard,
where the most demokratic combats, the counter-
summits,
have recourse to direct action,
A role awaits us.
That of the martyrs of the demokratic order,
which preventatively strikes every body that *might*
strike it.
I should sing the song of the victim. Since, we all
know,
everyone is a victim, even the oppressors.
And savor the masochism whose discrete circulation
makes the situation magical again.

Today, the human strike means
refusing to play the role of victim.
Attacking it.

Reappropriating violence.
Appropriating impunity.
Alerting the stoned citizenry
*that if they don't join in the war they are at war all
the same.*
That when ONE tells us it's either this or death, it's
always
actually
this *and* death.

So,
from human strike
to human strike, spread
the insurrection,
where there's nothing but,
where we are all,
whatever
singularities.

Notes

Introduction to Civil War

1. The French indefinite pronoun *on* is translated several ways depending on context: "it," "we," "they" and, at times, "one." The word appears frequently here in all capitals, indicating a special emphasis. We have on occasion decided to translate *ON* as "THEY." In doing so, we echo the conventions of certain French translators of Heidegger's *Being and Time*, who render *Das Man* by "l'On." Heidegger's English translators propose "the 'They.'" But this solution is inadequate, and at times we have simply used "ONE," in the sense of "someone."

2. Modeled in part after Leopold Bloom from James Joyce's *Ulysses*, "Bloom" is a conceptual persona who figures prominently in the work of Tiqqun. See in particular Tiqqun, *Theorie du Bloom* (Paris: La Fabrique, 2004), from which we extract a provisional description: "Last man, man on the street, man of the crowds, man of the masses, mass-man, this is how THEY have represented Bloom to us: as the sad product of the time of multitudes, as the catastrophic son of the industrial era and the end of enchantments. But in these designations we also feel a shudder, THEY tremble before the *infinite mystery of the ordinary man*. Everyone senses that the theater of his qualities hides *pure potentiality*: a pure power we are *supposed* to know nothing about" (16–17).

3. To be *polarisé* can mean to be obsessed with something or someone; more generally, it refers to the convergence of a field of energy or forces around a single point. When in English one speaks of a "polarizing" figure or event, it indicates the production of irreconcilable differences between groups or parties. Here, the

term evokes a process in which a body is affected by a form-of-life in such a way as to take on a charge that orients it in a specific manner: it is attracted by certain bodies, repulsed by others.

4. Émile Benveniste, *Le vocabulaire des institutions indo-européennes, tome 1* (Paris: Gallimard, 1966), 87, 92–94.

5. Immanuel Kant, *Practical Philosophy*, ed. Mary J. Gregor (Cambridge: Cambridge University Press, 1996), 328 [AK 8:357].

6. Sebastian Roché, *La societé d'hospitalité* (Paris: Seuil, 2000).

7. Friedrich Nietzsche, *The Gay Science*, trans. Josefine Nauckhoff (Cambridge: Cambridge University Press, 2001), 128.

8. "Whose realm, his religion"—a Latin expression meaning whoever is sovereign dictates the religion of the land.

9. *Publicité* is connected to the German *Öffentlichkeit* and means "public sphere" or "public opinion." The German root *offen-* suggests openness, clarity, transparency and manifestness. Yet instead of translating *publicité* as "public sphere," which carries specific connotations in political theory, we use "publicity," following the convention established by Kant's translators. Note however that "publicity" does not just mean advertising in a narrow sense, but rather the whole sphere of "publicness."

10. Thomas Hobbes, *Leviathan* (Indianapolis, IN: Hackett, 1994), 112.

11. See "On the Economy as Black Magic" *Tiqqun* 1 (1999).

12. Norbert Elias, *The Civilizing Process: Sociogenetic and Psychogenetic Investigations*, trans. Edmund Jephcott (Oxford: Blackwell, 1994), 375.

13. Hobbes, *Leviathan*, 219.

14. The quotation is probably a reference to one of the two following passages: "the simple compactness of their individuality has been shattered into a multitude of separate atoms," in G.W.F. Hegel, *Phenomenology of Spirit*, trans. A.V. Miller (Oxford: Oxford University Press, 1977), 289; or, "as a simple undifferentiated mass or as a crowd split up into atomic units," in G.W.F.

Hegel, *Elements of the Philosophy of Right*, trans. H. B. Nisbet (Cambridge: Cambridge University Press, 1991), 343.

15. Alexis de Tocqueville, *The Old Regime and the Revolution, Volume 1*, trans. Alan Kahan (Chicago: University of Chicago Press, 1998), 243, 242, 197, 198, 98.

16. The reference is to lines 24–28 of Hobbes' verse autobiography: "My native place I'm not ashamed to own; / Th'ill times, and ills born with me, I bemoan. / For fame had rumour'd that a fleet at sea, / Would cause our nation's catastrophe. / And hereupon it was my mother dear / Did bring forth twins at once, both me and fear" (Hobbes, *Leviathan*, liv).

17. Thomas Hobbes, *The Elements of Law, Natural and Politic: Human Nature and de Corpore Politico with Three Lives* (Oxford: Oxford University Press, 1999), 21, 59.

18. Hobbes, *Leviathan*, 76, 75.

19. Ibid., 77.

20. The phrase refers to the Rousseau text of the same name, "Que l'état de guerre naît de l'état social," in Jean-Jacques Rousseau, *Œuvres complètes, vol. III* (Paris: Gallimard, 1964), 601–612. The English translation is available in variant form as "The State of War," *Collected Writings of Rousseau, vol. 11*, trans. Christopher Kelly and Judith Bush (Hanover, NH: University Press of New England, 2005), 61–73.

21. Hobbes, *Leviathan*, 233.

22. Ibid., 77.

23. For these two essays see Pierre Clastres, *Archeology of Violence*, trans. Jeanine Herman (New York: Semiotext(e), 1994), 139–200.

24. Ibid., 166–167.

25. Hegel, *Elements of the Philosophy of Right*, 262–263.

26. "Tel est mon bon plaisir," a reference to "car tel est notre bon plaisir," the expression instituted by Francis I and used by monarchs when signing law.

27. Michel Foucault, *The Birth of Biopolitics: Lectures at the College de France, 1978–1979*, trans. Graham Burchell (New York: Palgrave Macmillan, 2008), 46.

28. Ibid., 67.

29. Ibid.

30. Michel Foucault, "The Crisis of Medicine or the Crisis of Antimedicine?" trans. Edgar C. Knowlton, Jr., et al., *Foucault Studies* 1 (December 2004): 5–19, 6.

31. Hobbes, *Leviathan*, 109.

32. Karl Marx, *Critique of Hegel's "Philosophy of Right"* (Cambridge: Cambridge University Press, 1977), 31, 32, emphasis Tiqqun.

33. Foucault, *The Birth of Biopolitics*, 46.

34. Michel Foucault, *Discipline and Punish: The Birth of the Prison*, trans. Alan Sheridan (New York: Vintage, 1977), 193.

35. "Faute blanche." This phrase can evoke "carte blanche" or "blank check." In these cases, the term "blanche" refers to something *unspecified*, a quantity of money or an offense, crime or "fault."

36. Antonio Negri, "L' 'Empire,' stade suprême de l'impérialisme," *Le Monde Diplomatique* (January, 2001): 3.

37. Thomas Hobbes, *De Cive* (Indianapolis, IN: Hackett, 1991), 250.

38. Michael Hardt and Antonio Negri, *Empire* (Cambridge, MA: Harvard University Press, 2000), xii, xi, 3.

39. Han Fei Tzu, *Complete Works of Han Fei Tzu, Vol. II*, trans. W. K. Liao (London: Arthur Probsthain, 1959), 229, 324. Some passages have been modified in accordance with the French translation Tiqqun uses.

40. Han Fei Tzu, *Complete Works of Han Fei Tzu, Vol. I*, trans. W. K. Liao (London: Arthur Probsthain, 1959), 58.

semiotext(e) intervention series

41. Ibid., 262.

42. Lao Tzu, *Tao Te Ching*, trans. D. C. Lau (New York: Knopf, 1994), 53.

43. Han Fei Tzu, *Complete Works of Han Fei Tzu*, Vol. I, 32–33, 34.

44. Ibid., 52–53, 54, 61.

45. Guy Brossollet, *Essai sur la non-bataille* (Paris: Belin, 1975), 78.

46. Friedrich Nietzsche, *Werke: Kritische Gesamtausgabe, VII* (Berlin: Walter de Gruyter, 1977), 541. This English translation is cited in Martin Heidegger, *Nietzsche, Vol 2*, trans. David Farrell Krell (New York: HarperCollins, 1991), 52.

47. Gilles Deleuze and Félix Guattari, *A Thousand Plateaus*, trans. Brian Massumi (Minneapolis: University of Minnesota Press, 1987), 423, emphasis removed.

48. Karl Marx, *The Civil War in France* (Chicago: Charles H. Kerr, 1998), 117.

49. Carl von Clausewitz, *On War*, trans. Michael Howard and Peter Paret (Princeton: Princeton University Press, 1976), 482, 480–481.

How Is It to Be Done?

1. A reference to Bernard Kouchner, co-founder of *Médecins du Monde*.

2. "Plague-carriers," a term used by the Italian Communist Party to describe Autonomia, and the subject of a 1977 issue of the journal *Recherches*, edited by Félix Guattari.